PRAISE FOR
SHUT UP AND LISTEN!

"Tilman's message isn't just for people in business. His approach to leadership, service, and knowing your strengths and weaknesses can be used by the most junior cadet or the most senior officer."

—Art Acevedo, President, Major Cities Chiefs
Association and Chief of Police, Houston, Texas

"You will want to reread and review Tilman's timeless lessons for business owners over and over again."

—Tom Brady, six-time Super Bowl Champion, four-
time Super Bowl MVP, three-time NFL MVP

"Tilman's swag comes through loud and clear on every page, telling you what you need to do to be successful."

—James Harden, NBA Houston Rockets All-Star and MVP

"Tilman offers up compelling lessons on how to build and run a business. If you want to rocket your business to new heights, this is the book for you."

—Scott Kelly, Capt. US Navy Retired, former NASA astronaut

"Take heed of every lesson and bit of advice dispensed in this groundbreaking and insightful book. Just as Tilman changed the University of Houston's trajectory, he can change yours too."

—Renu Khator, Chancellor, University of Houston
System and President, University of Houston

"Tilman doesn't just understand business—he understands what the customer wants because of his rare ability to see the world through other people's eyes."

—Michael Milken, Chairman, The Milken Institute

"Mr. Fertitta provides great insights to apply to the management of businesses, and people, that span all industries and all cultures."

—Yao Ming, business executive, former
Houston Rocket and NBA All-Star

"Once you instill the principles of this book into your mindset and culture, you will know success."

—Stephanie Ruhle, MSNBC anchor, *NBC News* business correspondent

"Tilman shares his secrets on how to succeed in a highly competitive marketplace, whether you're running a small business or operating a multibillion-dollar sports team."

—Adam Silver, Commissioner of the NBA

"I've seen Tilman's unique business strategies in action many times. All through the book he breaks them down in ways that are not only easy to understand, but can be used in any type of business."

—Brian Sullivan, CNBC anchor

SHUT
UP
AND
LISTEN!

SHUT UP AND LISTEN!

HARD BUSINESS TRUTHS
THAT WILL HELP YOU SUCCEED

TILMAN FERTITTA

HarperCollins
LEADERSHIP

AN IMPRINT OF HarperCollins

Published by HarperCollins Leadership, an imprint of HarperCollins
Focus LLC.

Published in association with One Street Books.

Any internet addresses, phone numbers, or company or product information
printed in this book are offered as a resource and are not intended in any
way to be or to imply an endorsement by HarperCollins Leadership, nor
does HarperCollins Leadership vouch for the existence, content, or services
of these sites, phone numbers, companies, or products beyond the life of
this book.

ISBN 978-1-4002-1374-0 (Ebook)
ISBN 978-1-4002-1373-3 (HC)

Library of Congress Control Number: 2019938796

Printed in the United States of America
19 20 21 22 23   LSC   10 9 8 7 6 5 4 3 2 1

CONTENTS

Foreword   ix

Acknowledgments   xiii

Introduction   xv

SECTION 1: HOSPITALITY ("IF THEY WANT SCRAMBLED EGGS . . .")

Chapter 1:   Hospitality Matters, No Matter the Business   3

Chapter 2:   Take the Word "No" Out of Your
             Damn Vocabulary   17

Chapter 3:   Cater to the Masses, Not the Classes   23

SECTION 2: YOU'D BETTER KNOW YOUR NUMBERS

Chapter 4:   Working Capital Is Everything   31

Chapter 5:   The Pitfalls of Property Leases   45

Chapter 6:   Know Your Numbers   51

SECTION 3: THE 95:5 RULE: WHAT'S YOUR "FIVE"?

Chapter 7:   Get to Know Your "Five"   61

Chapter 8:   Know and Leverage Your Strengths   71

Chapter 9:   Partner with Complementary Strengths   77

CONTENT

SECTION 4: SEE THE OPPORTUNITY, SEIZE THE OPPORTUNITY

Chapter 10: A Five-Year Reprieve   85
Chapter 11: "I Wonder If I'll Ever Have a Company
             That Does $10 Million in Sales"   93
Chapter 12: Don't Ever Lose the Hunger   101

SECTION 5: LIVE YOUR LEADERSHIP

Chapter 13: If You Want to Lead, Listen First   109
Chapter 14: Be a Great Teacher   119
Chapter 15: Change, Change, Change   129

Conclusion: Don't Choose to Quit—Choose
        to Keep Punching   141
Afterword: "Now That You've Listened . . ."   151
The Tilman I Know   157
About the Author   167

FOREWORD

Over the course of more than four decades, I have spent my career covering the greatest athletes and winners the world has ever seen, interviewing legends Muhammad Ali, Tom Brady, Michael Jordan, and Michael Phelps. The dedication, devotion, hard work, integrity, intellect, imagination, commitment to excellence, and heart have made them global icons.

The same principles apply in business. So I think I have an idea why you're reading this book. It's because you want to learn from an incredible winner in business.

Tilman Fertitta has risen to the top of the mountain and is one of the biggest winners in business history.

If you're a business professional, you may know Tilman as owner of Landry's Inc. and the many hotels, restaurants, and casinos they own and operate, or from his CNBC show, *Billion Dollar Buyer*. If you're a sports fan, you may know him as owner of the Houston Rockets, or for serving as chairman of the Board of Regents at the University of Houston, where he has helped build the institution and athletic program to prominence.

If you know Tilman personally, as I do, you know that he oversees his various businesses with a passion and energy that is just as strong today as it was when he opened his first restaurant over thirty-five years ago. Even with all of his success, his drive is like he just arrived at his first day on the job. There is no room for complacency working with Tilman, and no detail too small when it comes to the experience he provides to his customers. There is no question that Tilman knows what it takes to start and manage a successful business. He knows how to motivate those who work with him, and he leads by example. He instills confidence, and empowers people, to get the best out of them. He trusts himself, so he is able to trust those around him. In fact, there are very few people you could turn to who know what it takes to succeed in business more than Tilman.

In *Shut Up and Listen!*, Tilman shares his secrets and strategies that have made him so successful and does so in his blunt, humorous style that readers will love. He uncovers common blind spots that can trip up entrepreneurs, and offers proven strategies that will help them grow. I don't know many people who can say, as Tilman does in the introduction—"You may think you know what you're doing, but I'm going to show you what you don't know"—and be right.

I highly recommend *Shut Up and Listen!* The wisdom and actionable insights Tilman offers in this groundbreaking new book are a potent combination that business owners of all types will value long after their first read. It's a lifetime of business lessons presented by a man who is willing to share a map of how you can navigate in business, and join him on the victory platform.

Jim Gray
Hall of Fame, Emmy Award-
winning sports journalist,
reporter, and producer

ACKNOWLEDGMENTS

I could not have written this book without the support of my entire family. My parents, Vic and Joy, and Paige, Michael, Patrick, Blayne, and Blake, and my brothers Jay and Todd, have heard every "Tilmanism" in this book and more.

I would like to thank those who provided critical feedback during the writing and editing process for this book, including Patrick Fertitta, Michael Fertitta, Steve Scheinthal, Dancie Ware, Melissa Radovich, and Dash Kohlhausen. My editor Lavaille Lavette was the catalyst for this book and has been there every step of the way to make this book a success.

I particularly want to acknowledge my friends and contemporaries who took time to make contributions to the "Tilman I Know" section of this book, including Rich Handler, Dave Jacquin, Capt. Mark Kelly, Capt. Scott Kelly, Michael Milken, and Dr. Renu Khator.

Lastly, without the dedication of all of my Landry's, Golden Nugget, and Rockets employees, I would not have built my organization to what it is today, and there would not be a book to write. I often brag about how fortunate I am to have kept so many long-tenured employees. I take their dedication as the ultimate compliment. I particularly want to acknowledge the following executives, all of whom have been with me for approximately twenty years:

Andy Alexander	Julie Liebelt
Keith Beitler	Rick Liem
Jeff Cantwell	Scott Marshall
Kerri Carr	Mark Monsma
Howard Cole	Don Rakoski
Gerry Del Prete	Kelly Roberts
Rhonda DePaulis	Kathy Ruiz
Jim Dufault	Steve Scheinthal
Richard Flowers	Paul Schultz
Shah Ghani	Lynn Small
Steve Greenberg	Dena Stagner
Nicki Keenan	Stephanie Tallent
Brett Kellerman	Karim Tamir
Lori Kittle	Terry Turney
James Kramer	Tim Whitlock

There is not enough space on the page to list the hundreds of other employees who have been with me so many years, but to all of you who were not listed on this page, thank you as well for your dedication.

INTRODUCTION

I f you are in business, want to start a business, or perhaps want to climb the corporate ladder, you've come to the right place. Now, shut up and listen to make that business all that it can possibly be.

I'm Tilman Fertitta. According to the Forbes 400 list, I'm ranked the 153rd richest person in America. As the sole owner and founder of Fertitta Entertainment, my organization owns and operates restaurants, hotels, amusement parks, and aquariums. You may be familiar with some of my restaurant brands, including Mastro's, Morton's The Steakhouse, Rainforest Café, Chart House, Bubba Gump Shrimp Co., Landry's Seafood House, Saltgrass Steak House, and thirty-five other concepts. In all, I own more than six hundred restaurants. I also own five Golden Nugget casinos and hotels. If that wasn't enough, I've also starred in my own reality show called *Billion Dollar Buyer* on CNBC.

Oh, by the way, if you didn't know, I also own the NBA's Houston Rockets.

That's a long way from starting with a single restaurant in Katy, Texas. And in this book, I want to share some of the key ideas and strategies I used to build an entertainment and hospitality empire that covers the globe.

To do that, I'd like to begin with a warning:

Be just like me: never, ever stop worrying about your business.

Why?

Because when it comes to business and most everything else in life, there is a paddle for everybody's ass.

And you never know when it's coming or where it's coming from.

I really do believe that. I don't care if things are going well for you, that you think you know it all. Put this one thing in your head: there is a paddle coming for your ass right now.

By a paddle, I mean that there is always a force out there, something that's taking square aim at your business's success and growth. There might be someone with a better product. There might be a lawsuit waiting to pounce. The economy may turn. A bank that you relied on may deny you credit. New government regulations may be ready to take effect. Your computer may be hacked. These days, it's not ridiculous to worry about a terrorist attack, international or domestic.

The best you can hope for when something damaging or disruptive happens is that you act quickly to minimize the impact. But you have to open your eyes. You need to start worrying, anticipating, planning, and being proactive. Why? Because the paddle comes from the blind spots we all have when we juggle the many roles and skill sets needed to successfully run a business.

It is way too easy for complacency and overconfidence to set in, which leads to ignoring crucial details.

"You might think you know what you're doing, but I'm going to show you what you don't know."

People ask me all the time: "What do you fear?" I say I don't fear anything, but I *worry* about everything. That's one of the significant features of the message I try to get across when I speak to business leaders, students, my employees, and entrepreneurs on my television show *Billion Dollar Buyer*. I have to tell entrepreneurs that, even as they pitch some very appealing products to me, there is some area where they are falling short that is hurting their business.

So, as the title of this book says, the next step is a simple one: Shut up and listen.

I've got a lot I'd like to share with you. And you'll be glad that you paid attention.

The book is divided into five sections, each of which talks about a core area that can kill a business if you're not aware of those blind spots. Here they are, in order:

1. Hospitality ("If They Want Scrambled Eggs . . .")
2. You'd Better Know Your Numbers

3. The 95:5 Rule: What's Your "Five"?
4. See the Opportunity, Seize the Opportunity
5. Live Your Leadership

Each section provides specific strategies and ideas to help your business break through to that next level. And if I want to emphasize something, it appears in a "Listen!" sidebar.

When it comes to business, it's absolutely critical to always remain realistic—about your product, your competition, and yourself. Be cognizant of everything you do and every decision you consider. This book will help you better analyze your strengths and weaknesses and understand what actions you should take. Be honest with yourself about all that you don't know—and what you can do about it. (As I like to say, I'm not about to go on the court and teach NBA MVP James Harden how to shoot a jump shot!)

I'll share some of the most straightforward strategies and ideas I've used in my own businesses and that you can use as well. These strategies will help you achieve the sort of breakout success that you want, no matter if you're just starting your business career or you're years into it.

Each chapter wraps up with what I call "Tilman's Targets"—a quick, easy-to-reference summary of major points that were covered in the chapter. They're a handy way to refer back to key concepts.

At the end of the book, I've included bonus content with a feature called "The Tilman I Know." You'll hear from several friends of mine who have their own thoughts about who I am and some of the things I've done to achieve success.

This isn't a textbook. These are the strategies I've used—in both good times and bad. As I'll discuss later, I've been through more than my share of days when it seemed like the whole world was falling apart. Having these ideas in mind helped keep me from throwing in the towel when it would have been the easiest thing in the world to do.

The fundamental concepts I'm sharing helped me succeed. In business there are no Oscars, Grammys, or Pro Bowl, but there is the Forbes 400 list, and I'm on it. I believe my ideas and strategies can help you achieve success no matter what sort of business you happen to be in. If you want to make money in business, you need to read this book.

Despite all my success, I walk around every day making sure that the paddle doesn't get my ass. I can take a few taps, but I don't want a big swat.

Neither do you.

So, saying this in the nicest way possible: "Shut up and listen!"

Let's get started.

SECTION 1
HOSPITALITY ("IF THEY WANT SCRAMBLED EGGS . . .")

Every successful business, in one way or another, is built around hospitality.

The problem is, many businesses fail to see that. And if they do, they don't pay nearly as much attention to it as they should.

Hospitality can mean everything to the success or failure of your business. In this section, I'll discuss what hospitality involves, why it means so much to your business, and how to overcome obstacles that can get in the way of providing hospitality—consistently and without exception.

CHAPTER 1

HOSPITALITY MATTERS, NO MATTER THE BUSINESS

We've all been there. And it's the kind of experience that drives us all absolutely crazy.

Probably because it happens. A lot.

It's 11:02 a.m. Maybe you've been in an important meeting or just arrived from the airport, but you walk into a restaurant, and you want some scrambled eggs.

Here's what you might hear. Take your pick:

"Sorry, we stopped serving breakfast at eleven."

"We serve eggs only at breakfast."

"The kitchen is shifting over to lunch."

"Sir, if you'd only been able to get here fifteen minutes sooner . . ."

No matter how it comes out of someone's mouth, the basic answer is the same:

Can't help you.

As I said, everybody has had to deal with this. And, as I also said, it can drive you crazy. You're not asking the kitchen to make you a waffle, pancakes, or even eggs Benedict. You're not asking them for an order of bacon (although they probably have some sitting over on a counter that they can heat up in a few minutes and toss into a club sandwich).

All you're asking for is someone in the kitchen to pick up a skillet, put it on the burner, and cook up a couple of scrambled eggs. But the server treats you as if you were trying to place an order for Peking duck—from scratch, prepared by a chef flown in nonstop from Beijing.

Maybe you try to argue with the staff about throwing a couple of eggs into a pan. Maybe you shrug and ask to see the lunch menu.

Or maybe you walk out and try to find someplace else to eat.

That's because something like this should never, ever happen.

But it does happen, all the time—and in different ways. You may telephone a hardware store with an important question, only to hear that everyone's busy. "Can you call back?"

Or maybe you're in a department store and ask if they have a particular wallet in stock. "No." Not a suggestion that they'd be happy to show you some similar items—just no.

Can the doctor take a few minutes to talk about your lab results? "Make an appointment."

For me, these are all a question of hospitality. And customer service and hospitality are everything, no matter what the business is.

To me, the definition of hospitality is simple. It's however you handle a customer. Nothing more, nothing less—how you treat him or her, how you respond to what he or she asks for, and your ability (and willingness) to stay flexible. The ultimate goal of interacting with a customer is to make him or her feel like the only customer you have in the entire world. Why? Because as I tell my own employees, there are no spare customers.

LISTEN!

It starts with how you talk with them. And you don't need to memorize any special words or magic sentences. The rule is simple: when talking to a customer, be sure to make the conversation all about them. Let them talk about their needs, what they hope to get out of buying your product or service. If they want to complain, listen. They want to be heard more than anything. Since you're trying to make them feel like they're the only customer you have, act like it. When dealing with that one customer, no one or nothing else matters at that moment.

If you want to boil it down even further, I have a rule of thumb that I say almost every day: it's free to be nice.

Think about that. As a business owner or entrepreneur, does it cost you anything to be courteous to each and every customer? Of course not! Being nice costs you nothing. But, by the same token, remember: it can cost you a hell of a lot to be rude.

Sometimes it's not the easiest thing in the world to be nice, no matter how much sense it may make from a business standpoint. Maybe your spouse or significant other said something that upset you right before you left for work. Maybe something else is going on in your life that makes it awfully difficult to be nice and cheery with each and every customer you deal with.

"Be plappy."

To which I have a simple answer: be plappy.

By that I mean "play happy." No matter how upset or worried you may be about other things in your life at the moment, do everything within your power to project a happy mood when you're on the job.

That's an ever-present rule of thumb at all of my businesses. When you step foot inside one of my businesses and you work for me, be plappy if you have to. One reason is that, as I said earlier, no one cares that your dog chewed up a $300 pair of shoes or that you have to meet with your kid's principal after work. That's reality.

The other reason that rule always stays in place in my businesses is that the customer experience is all that matters. We're in the hospitality business, so we have to be sure to be hospitable all the time.

And no matter the specifics of what you do, you're in the hospitality business as well.

Follow-through is another aspect of hospitality. For example, if you say you're going to deliver the product on the thirteenth at three o'clock, deliver it exactly at that time. Don't call minutes before it is due and say it's going to be three days later than you had planned. Even worse, don't call after the product was due to be delivered and say it's going to be even later. (Your customer already knows that, by the way.)

Just as important, don't offer up an excuse to explain the delay. Nobody cares that your driver's kid got sick and he had to pick him up early from school. Not to sound mean or heartless, but somebody who orders something from you doesn't care that your mother-in-law died.

I'm sorry your child got sick. My condolences for your mother-in-law's passing. But if I'm a customer who was told that a product I ordered would arrive on such and such a date and at such and such a time, all I'm focused on is the fact that something I was expecting—maybe something very important to me—isn't going to arrive as planned.

We all have kids who get sick. Relatives and loved ones pass away. Personal problems crop up daily. You know that, and so do I. But a promise to a customer should be treated as something that shouldn't be affected by the sorts of problems and unexpected events we all deal with constantly. Business would be a whole lot easier if life never got in the way, but it does.

There's a simple way to address this problem. Try building in a few what-ifs. When you make a promise to a customer, take into account that something may go wrong or get in the way of keeping your commitment. Assume a worst-case scenario. Tack on a few extra hours or even days to give yourself a little cushion.

One way I do this is by being very careful about how I schedule my time. I generally avoid making commitments too far in advance. For me, I never build a schedule that's longer than a couple of weeks or a month out. That way, if something comes up during that time frame, I've given myself enough time to find a work-around. You're focused but also flexible.

That sets you up for a win-win. Either you deliver the product as planned or, even better, you call your customer and say the product came in earlier than expected.

If you offer a due date that the customer feels is too far away, now is the time to explain why it has to be that way. It's not an excuse; it's an explanation. And from the customer's standpoint, an explanation of why something is going to take as long as it will to arrive is easier to accept than some sort of excuse later regarding its slow delivery. When you make an excuse, you're basically asking a customer for forgiveness because you didn't deliver as promised.

The overall goal is to make certain a customer feels special. And a customer who feels special will bring you more business and tell all of her friends how much she loves your service.

Of course, there will be times when things don't go as planned. Maybe a delivery is going to be late, or something on the menu isn't to your customer's complete satisfaction. It's critical to make that misstep up to the customer in some way.

In our businesses, we have lots of things at our disposal. For instance, if five people are eating dinner at a table, and one diner gets his meal ten minutes after the others, we'll likely comp that meal. If someone stays at one of our hotels or resorts and has a negative experience, we may offer them a free night's stay so that we can show them how we do things right.

But it's also a balancing act. If someone spends fifty dollars and is unhappy, we're certainly not going to give her something worth $300 to make it up to her. Not only is that completely out of balance, but it's an exaggerated apology. While you want to right the wrong, you may inadvertently be making something out to be a bigger deal than it actually is.

It circles back to making certain the customer knows you're listening. Ask questions and react accordingly. And resolve the problem as quickly as possible, so it doesn't turn into a monster.

Keep in mind also that there will be times when a dissatisfied customer is being unreasonable. There are people who will sit down at a restaurant, eat an entire steak, and then complain that it was overcooked.

First, be nice and respectful, no matter what you may be thinking about that particular customer. Then, remind the customer that he, in fact, did polish off the entire steak. Had he said something earlier, you could have done something, possibly replacing the steak with another meal. But since he did eat the whole thing, the only logical thing for you to conclude was that the steak was perfectly fine. In a nutshell, maintain a balanced, polite demeanor while you're explaining that there's nothing else you can do.

Is that telling a customer no? In a way, it is. In this instance, it's the honest response and the only one that makes business sense.

"Build a few hours or days into your schedule for the what-ifs. If I tell somebody I'm going to deliver something on this day, I'm damn well going to deliver it. I'm going to make that customer feel special."

Speaking of business sense, let's apply a what-if to the scrambled eggs story that opened this chapter. The best what-if would be a kitchen that sets aside a few eggs and other breakfast items to accommodate late arrivals. What if the kitchen has some quiches all made and ready to stand in for scrambled eggs?

Or, even more simply, what if the server took your order, and the kitchen staff tossed a couple of eggs into a pan and made a couple slices of toast? They may very well charge you twenty-five dollars for an eggs and toast breakfast, but that's what you wanted. (Remember, there's a big segment of the population that would say I don't give a crap how much it costs—I just want scrambled eggs!)

More to the point, by building in a what-if strategy, or by being flexible, you've made a customer feel special. And that's the overriding goal of hospitality.

But don't lose sight of the fact that you're a businessperson.

Bust your rear to make certain that a customer never hears no, but that every action makes business sense as well. You're in business to make money. A customer wants scrambled eggs. Make them for him but charge for the additional effort. If they want scrambled eggs at 8:00 p.m., charge for them. If a customer wants expedited delivery or something installed at their home, be smart. Know what your costs are and charge them accordingly. Not only will you have a happy customer, you're also taking care of yourself as a businessperson.

This raises an important point. Nobody's product is that great. Nobody's product is so amazing that it stands out completely from everything else. You may have a perfectly good product, but you're competing against a bunch of other perfectly good products. That's the reality of business.

How you can separate yourself from the competition is through hospitality—attention to customer needs and wants, 24/7. Think about the same two products—one is delivered on time as promised, and one arrives one day late. You tell me what that customer is going to remember.

Hospitality is essential to all sorts of businesses. I don't care if you're a doctor—you should be a hospitable doctor and have a great bedside manner. If you think about it, every doctor around can give you the exact same flu shot. The one who helps you relax, so the shot doesn't hurt like hell, is the one you're going to go back to.

I was talking with someone not long ago who sees a therapist regularly. The appointment is always over at three o'clock sharp. Out the door she goes. Almost anybody who sees a therapist can relate to that sort of rigid schedule. Feeling better? Good. Please pay at the next available window. Next patient! Keep it moving!

What would happen if that therapist built in a little extra time for each session that the patient could use if he or she wanted to? One time they might go over by seven minutes, another by three minutes. What would happen if a masseuse you book for an hour's massage actually spent sixty minutes with you, rather than showing you the door after fifty minutes, after starting five minutes late?

The point isn't so much that the therapy is any more effective—although it might be—but that the patient feels as though the therapist really cares. She doesn't feel as though she's being thrown out of the office at exactly the same time. She truly feels like she matters, that her therapist is ready to give her extra attention if she feels she needs it.

That's hospitality—a patient who doesn't feel like just another name on a chart.

LISTEN!

Hospitality not only applies to every business—it also applies across every part of that business. Everyone working for a business, no matter what they do, should practice hospitality with the same level of commitment as everybody else.

Here's how that can play out. You go out to dinner, and you're promptly escorted to your table. You're waited on by a courteous and helpful server. The food is outstanding, as is the dessert that follows. You leave as a thoroughly happy customer.

But it all falls apart when you try to get your car. Maybe the valet misplaces your keys. Maybe it takes the valet sixteen minutes to find where he parked your car. Maybe when the valet drives up with your car, you notice a scratch on the driver's side door that wasn't there when you dropped it off.

All of a sudden, the memory of that great experience you had at the restaurant is completely gone. After a great meal and great service, you drive home pissed off because of the service the valet offered.

But is that great experience really gone? Maybe not. The issue isn't necessarily limited to the valet's mistake. The issue is, did your general manager talk to the valet? Did the valet bring it to the restaurant's attention? And then what did the restaurant do to help alleviate the situation? Did they ask the customer to sit down and talk, to address what happened and, just as important, to ask what can be done to make him or her feel better about their experience?

Problems are inevitable. What matters is what you can do to make that customer happy again or, at the very least, mitigate the bad experience. Put another way, sometimes you can't avoid the fire. It's how you put it out that matters.

The same can happen in any business. A patient leaving a therapist's office after the doctor gave him or her a few extra minutes can be turned off by a moody receptionist.

That's all part of being in the hospitality business. It involves everyone and depends on everyone. It's called taking care of your customer. And, if even one person forgets that, an otherwise great customer experience can go straight down the drain. So be ready to respond when that happens. And believe me, it will happen.

Sometimes, a lapse in hospitality occurs by a matter of choice—the most unforgivable mistake, in my estimation.

Here's what I mean. I was staying at a five-star hotel in Chicago a while ago. At the end of a very long day, some associates and I went down to the bar to unwind and have a drink. As we were relaxing and enjoying our drinks, the bartender came up to us and asked us to leave.

Why? Because the cleaning crew wanted to get started cleaning the bar!

I have a saying that bartenders love to run your bars, but this went way beyond anything I could have ever imagined. Can you imagine going to a five-star hotel and having some drinks and then being asked to clear out because the cleaning crew wanted to start vacuuming? Is that being hospitable? On a more practical level, was that the only space that needed cleaning? Could they have gone somewhere else while we finished our drinks at our own pace?

This example highlights the importance of telling everyone with whom you work that hospitality comes before everything else. Make hospitality the forefront of everything your business does, from making certain that deliveries arrive as promised to feeding a hungry customer just what he wants, no matter the hour. And, in the case of my cocktail at the Chicago hotel, hospitality means doing things at the customer's convenience, not your own.

Take hospitality personally. When I'm in one of my restaurants, and I see someone get a drink without a napkin, or food that's not hot or that's on the wrong plate, it bothers me to my core. I truly look at it as a reflection and a representation of myself.

And, if you go into one of my restaurants at eight o'clock at night, there are going to be scrambled eggs there if you want them. I may charge you more, but you're a happy customer who got what you asked for.

TILMAN'S TARGETS

- Make hospitality your goal, no matter what business you're in.
- Hospitality means making a customer feel special.
- Keep your promises. Build in what-ifs to help you follow through on your commitments.
- Make hospitality the goal for everyone involved in your business. One person who doesn't show hospitality can ruin an otherwise positive customer experience.

CHAPTER 2

TAKE THE WORD "NO" OUT OF YOUR DAMN VOCABULARY

For years, I've had a question stuck in my head. And no matter how hard I try, I can never come up with a good answer:

Why is it so easy to say no when you can say yes to a customer?

That's a simple question but, as I said, I've never come across what I would consider a fair answer.

In the world of business, particularly for entrepreneurs and businesses just starting out, it would seem to be such an easy question to answer. A customer asks for something, and you say, "Yes, no problem." End of story.

But in many ways, businesses say no to customers all the time. And it's one hell of a mistake.

It can be as simple as saying you can't make a customer

scrambled eggs after 11:00 a.m., like the example in the previous chapter. With my experience in the hotel business, it can be as simple as telling a customer he can't have his suit cleaned and back to him by the next morning, since he missed the deadline by thirty minutes.

Sometimes saying no to a customer has a higher price than pissing off someone who would be happy if you just said yes. Say a customer asks to substitute shrimp for oysters. I know for a fact they cost you the same. Charge a substitution fee, but don't tell them no.

"Why is it so easy to say no when you can say yes?"

I really can't say why this sort of thing happens—a casual attitude toward work maybe, or a sense that customers tolerate more these days—but there's an easy solution to all this: take the word *no* out of your damn vocabulary.

I preach that all the time. Never, ever say no to a customer. And there are plenty of reasons never to say no beyond the obvious one that you might alienate an otherwise happy customer.

LISTEN!

If you think about it, saying no to a customer usually doesn't mean that you can't do something. Instead, you're choosing not to do something.

That's a big difference. Obviously, in some situations you can't do something. Say your business is scheduled to make a delivery to a retailer, but a major storm is flooding roads everywhere. In that instance, telling your customer you're going to be late is understandable. No one can control the weather.

And, in some cases, what a customer asks for can be completely unreasonable. In all fairness, not every customer is going to ask for something that's realistic, like the customer who asks for a refund after devouring an entire steak. When that happens, saying yes can be hard to do.

But in far many more instances, saying no translates to someone saying they choose not to do what the customer asks.

Let's go back to the scrambled eggs example from chapter 1. A customer wants scrambled eggs, but it's way past breakfast time. The server says they can't make scrambled eggs.

Wait a minute. Is the kitchen out of eggs? Are all the skillets dirty? Have the chickens gone on strike?

Of course not. Everything's there to make a perfectly good plate of scrambled eggs. Yet the restaurant is choosing to say no to a customer.

Believe it or not, I think customers pick up on this much more than you might imagine. They know full well that when someone says, "I can't," it really means "I won't." Think about that. How would you feel if a business told you no, pretty much because they didn't feel like doing it, not because it was beyond their ability to agree to what you asked for?

That's a bad situation to put yourself in. First off, customers who hear no are made to feel as though they're expendable, that their business doesn't matter. I like to say there are no spare customers, and saying no to one is a certain way to make them feel unimportant, fast. Don't put yourself in a position to tell your customer no. If you run out of ice cream, hamburger buns, tomatoes, whatever, go to the damn grocery store and get some. You can tell your customer you're out of Wagyu beef, but not something you can get at a grocery store down the street.

"There are no spare customers."

I also like to say it's essential to treat every customer like he or she is the only one you have. But saying no to someone can make him or her feel like a number, just another item on the list. With just one word—no—you can be telling that customer, "I'm saying no to you because you really don't matter."

It's also important to bear in mind that when you wipe the word *no* out of your customer vocabulary, that doesn't necessarily mean you have to say an outright yes. Offer alternatives, a sort of "I can't do that for you, sir, but I can do this." If a customer likes your product in a particular color that you don't happen to have, suggest a color close to it. If your restaurant is out of a menu item that a customer orders, offer her a discount to come back the next night, when she can get the food she wants. You're not telling them no—instead, it's a qualified yes.

In short, say what you *can* do, not what you can't.

That's an important message to get across. Even if you can't meet the customer's exact request, you're showing a willingness to do something else to keep him or her happy. Again, it's a matter of choice—you're choosing to take those extra steps to make someone feel special and valued.

Taking the word *no* out of your vocabulary also encourages you and anyone else with whom you work to think on your feet. In many ways, saying no is the easy way out of a situation. But if you refuse to say no, you often have to come up with some alternatives quickly. That can build a business that's responsive and flexible in all sorts of ways. (Later, I discuss the importance of thinking on your feet.)

All this may seem very simple, and it is. But you'd be shocked at how many businesses with great products and services inadvertently shoot themselves in the foot by telling customers no in all sorts of ways. However, if you're aware of it and make a consistent, conscious effort to never tell a customer no, you're going to see results.

You don't always need to say yes to a customer. But never saying no may be one of the most valuable strategies you can use to help your business break out to the next level.

TILMAN'S TARGETS

- Never tell a customer no.
- There are no spare customers.
- Understand the difference between being unable to

do something for a customer and choosing not to do something.

- If you can't say yes, offer alternatives.
- Never saying no encourages you and everyone involved in your business to think on their feet.

CHAPTER 3

CATER TO THE MASSES, NOT THE CLASSES

One of the biggest obstacles an entrepreneur can face is believing that his or her product is the only one like it anywhere in the world. As I've said before, that's completely unrealistic.

But that reality can also raise an issue that's a problem for any business looking to grow—a product that's too narrow to attract wide interest.

If you want your business to break out to the next level, cater to the masses, not the classes. The math behind that is simple. The broader the appeal of the products or services you sell, the more customers you will have. And that starts by doing what the customer dictates you should do.

A lot of people run their businesses according to how they

think it should be done. They base their products, services, and much of the customer experience on what they like—be it food, service, or some other element. The problem is that you can't do what you like. Granted, you may have a great idea or product you absolutely love, but whether you love it or not is largely beside the point. You may like liver, but can you build a restaurant chain around liver? Not likely. To build your business, you want to do what the masses like.

Pay close attention to the feedback you receive. Your customers will be telling you what they do and don't like, in so many words. And by listening to what they have to say, you're not consciously limiting your potential customer base. Instead, you're working toward making it as large as possible.

First is the obvious question of price. Is your product or service priced to be within reach of the greatest number of people possible, while still giving you a sufficient margin? If your product is priced too high, you may be losing customers who otherwise might be attracted to what you have to offer them. That's an unnecessarily small target.

There are all sorts of ways to identify a solid price point. Start with knowing who your competitors are. It may be surprising to learn, but many entrepreneurs don't clearly understand who their actual competitors are. For instance, someone who's offering a different product or service can be as challenging a competitor as someone doing the exact same thing as you. When looking at potential competitors, watch for products and services that someone may buy instead of yours, identical and otherwise. When talking with customers, take a minute to ask where else they've looked. Ignoring or overlooking a key competitor can be devastating.

Next, see what your competitors are selling and at what price. There are plenty of resources available regarding industry standards that you can refer to. Use them as a guide but not as gospel. By knowing your numbers—such as production costs, labor, and others—you'll begin to see what, if any, adjustments to those prices you should make to help your business become both more profitable and accessible to the most customers.

This is as common a problem as I've seen in all sorts of businesses. Entrepreneurs routinely price their products higher than they should if they want to attract a wide range of customers. And that goes for wholesale as well as retail. Wholesalers expect deeply discounted prices by buying in quantity, yet entrepreneurs often ask for prices that are anything but discounts. Sometimes that's a production issue—decreasing production costs always translates to lower prices—and sometimes an inexperienced entrepreneur hasn't been exposed to the sorts of discounts that major wholesale buyers can command.

Price is just part of what you need to take into account. For instance, does age come into play? Is your product or service attractive to a person of a certain age, or does it appeal to customers whose ages range across the board? Does that include kids and teenagers? What about college-aged kids and postgraduate millennials?

What about gender? Is yours a male- or female-only product, or might anyone be interested? Go through these questions with an idea of expanding the appeal of your product.

One way to look at the challenge of catering to the masses is to approach it like a restaurant menu. Of course, some restaurants don't exactly cater to the budget-minded among us—or, for that matter, don't include children or diners with particular dietary needs among their target market. That's perfectly okay.

But a restaurant that's aiming for a wide audience knows how that goal should be reflected in its menu. More affordable sandwiches and small dishes can complement higher-priced items. A kid's menu targets the younger diner, while giving mom and dad a price break. Gluten-free, vegetarian, vegan, and other options cater to customers with particular diets.

You get the idea. Offering customers a wide range of choices is one proven way to cater to the masses.

With that in mind, consider the products or services your business currently offers. What could you add to that "menu" that might attract a broader customer range? What products or services would naturally complement what you already sell? For instance, if you're selling your grandmother's homemade pasta recipe, can you introduce other flavors or other fillings? How about her from-scratch tomato sauce to accompany the pasta? What seems like a natural add-on?

If more products aren't the answer, or even possible, what can you do to make what you already have more appealing to more customers? That could be as simple as broadening the range of colors or varying the material used for a particular item. Can a product be used for something other than what it was originally intended to do?

The point here is to always stretch your thinking, to see

beyond the obvious. Look at what you have and explore any ways you can add to it or reframe it so that more customers will sit up and take notice.

I'm not saying that you can't sell an exclusive product or something geared to a specific audience. That's fine. But if you want to attract the sort of financial response you need to help your business break out, it's always a solid idea to try to engage with the biggest audience you possibly can.

That's because, particularly for entrepreneurs and small, emerging businesses, you want to sell to the masses, not the classes. Businesses that cater to the masses inevitably end up making more money than those that limit their scope.

TILMAN'S TARGETS

- Cater to the masses, not the classes.
- Work to make your product appealing to as broad an audience as possible.
- Understand your competition.
- Know your target audience.

YOU'D BETTER KNOW YOUR NUMBERS

One overriding factor determines whether any business is destined to rise to the next level or struggle endlessly: your numbers.

This is something I emphasize not only in my own businesses—as I like to say, ask me anything about my businesses, and I'll be able to answer you—but to entrepreneurs of all sorts. You need to know your numbers, and you need to know them cold.

If you ask me why I've been successful, I usually break it down into four reasons:

1. I know my numbers.
2. I understand operations.

3. I know the developmental side (i.e., how to grow your business).

4. I change, change, change with the times.

Of those four, knowing your numbers is by far the most important piece of all.

The reasons are simple yet powerful. The numbers drive everything that happens in your business—what you have coming in, what you have going out, and the critical interaction between the two. And if you don't know your numbers—and by "know," I mean right down to the specific decimal points—you're likely headed for trouble.

Just as important, a failure to know your numbers can needlessly handicap your business's growth. Without sufficient cash on hand, you may find yourself passing up opportunities that you might have otherwise pursued. Or you might make financial decisions and commitments that you later regret.

I don't care how great a product or service you have. If you don't know your numbers, you'll go out of business.

Don't let that happen.

CHAPTER 4

WORKING CAPITAL IS EVERYTHING

E very number that has to do with your business is undeniably important. But one financial reality is of particular importance to small businesses looking to scale.

LISTEN!

For a small business or an entrepreneur, working capital can mean the difference between success and extinction.

Many entrepreneurs have a dangerously simple idea of how business works. To them, it's very straightforward—you sell something to someone else, and you get paid. End of story.

Except that's not even close to how things work.

Here's an example of what I'm getting at. Let's say an entrepreneur designs an absolutely beautiful purse—stylish and eye-catching at the same time. She takes a sample around to various high-end retail outlets, and the product is appealing enough to attract immediate attention from the store owners.

"You know what?" says one. "I'd like to carry those in my store. I'll take thirty-six. When can you deliver them?"

That's a problem. The entrepreneur is thrilled with the order but lacks the necessary cash to buy the materials to produce thirty-six purses. And after the purses are manufactured and delivered, the store placing the order can have a month or longer to pay for them, according to most current accounts payable standards.

That's an issue that I see over and over again with all sorts of entrepreneurs. They expect to be paid right away, only to discover that the money they rely on to keep things operating isn't going to arrive for a month and a half.

What do they run out of? Working capital. And in my experience, the number one reason—by far—that people don't make it is because of working capital.

"The biggest issue that small businesses face involves working capital, because they have to pay for everything up front."

Breaking down the topic a bit, working capital is the difference between a company's current assets and liabilities. Current assets are those that can be turned into cash within the next twelve months; liabilities are expenses, costs, and other charges within that same twelve-month time frame.

Working capital is well named. That's because it's money you can put to use right away to help your business function at its peak all the time.

A company's working capital situation is determined by a number of factors. For instance, some businesses require more working capital than others, such as manufacturers that need funds to buy supplies necessary to make products.

How long it takes to make those products is known as the business's operating cycle—the longer the cycle, the greater the need for cash on hand. Operating cycle also refers to the situation I described earlier: the entrepreneur who makes a sale but has to wait several weeks to be paid. That's a gap that needs to be filled.

Then there's the sort of business in question. For example, if you have a business that's cyclical in nature—you have certain busy seasons or have products geared to particular holidays— you're going to need plenty of working capital. That's money that will not only see you through leaner portions of the year but also help you gear up as you approach peak seasons.

Christmas is an ideal example. Many retail businesses experience a significant sales spike during the holiday shopping season. Yet many struggle since they don't have the working capital necessary to stock up for the holidays.

Working capital also fuels growth. If a small-business owner or entrepreneur starts a business and wants to expand it, they'll need lots of working capital to fund that expansion. On the other hand, someone with more modest goals may be perfectly happy to stay small, requiring less cash.

These and other issues are the sorts of things that never occur to many entrepreneurs—until the day they find they lack the necessary cash to meet even the most basic expenses, let alone have the money to grow.

If you think about it, that creates something of an uneven playing field. Many small businesses have to pay for essential expenses up front, only to find that the same sort of quick payment doesn't happen when customers place an order. Unfair maybe, but that's the way it is.

Sometimes the worst thing that can happen to a small business is sudden success—by success, I mean a large number of orders. On the surface that may seem like the best thing that can happen, but without working capital available to produce the products to fill those orders, all you may end up with is a rash of unfilled orders and angry, disappointed customers.

Even having a large number of assets won't necessarily cover for a lack of ready cash. The infamous Enron story is a perfect example. Enron went under due to a lack of liquidity and working capital. They had billions in assets, which they didn't have time to sell to pay those basic expenses I mentioned earlier. Their assets were eventually divvied up and sold off after the company went under. With billions in assets, they didn't have to fail, but they did because they didn't have sufficient working capital.

So, what's the answer? Every business needs a "revolver," meaning a revolving line of credit, such as a bridge loan or line of credit, to fill in the gap.

The trouble is, getting a line of credit or loan can be difficult, particularly for a new business. Banks have been cutting back on their financing of small businesses, particularly larger banks. And as smaller community banks are swallowed up by larger institutions, the number of choices available to borrow from is growing smaller all the time.

I know exactly what this feels like. When I was starting out, I tried to get my hands on money in every possible way I could—credit cards, you name it. (One thing I didn't do was reach out to friends for loans. If you want to lose a friend, just ask for a loan. Nothing destroys a friendship faster.)

Add to that the fact that, at the time, the banking environment in Houston and throughout Texas was being shaken to its core as bank after bank shut its doors (a situation that, as it turned out, worked in my favor, as I describe in a later chapter), so securing working capital was nearly impossible.

Even though the banking situation is a good deal more stable now, it can still be difficult for entrepreneurs and small-business owners to get financial help from a bank. Often, new businesses have little in the way of operating history to support their credit worthiness or collateral to borrow against, so their inability to secure loans isn't all that surprising. Many lenders will give lines of credit only to companies that have a minimum of two years' worth of operating history.

Start by building up your cash reserves. This is separate from bank financing but is a critical step to ensure you have as much liquidity as possible. It's important for entrepreneurs to understand that business cycles go up and down. Be prepared for the down cycle. During down cycles, use your cash to expand your business. But during boom cycles, save cash for the next downturn.

"When things are bad, eat the weak
and grow your business."

That's not just a matter of survival. It gives you the opportunity to eat the weak and grow your business—while others are struggling mightily.

Here's an example of what I'm getting at. Lake Charles, Louisiana, may not be a familiar city, but it's the primary gaming market for my hometown of Houston, Texas—the oil capital of the world and fourth-largest city in the United States. Owning a casino in Lake Charles was something I had my eye on for a long, long time, because I knew I could do a bunch of business there by bringing in my unparalleled hospitality, which everyone in Houston already knew.

The problem was that no more available gaming licenses were available in Louisiana, making getting into that market very unlikely. Or so I thought.

Out of nowhere, on May 29, 2013, the Federal Trade Commission (FTC) announced that a casino in Lake Charles that was being built by Ameristar Casinos (which was being acquired by Pinnacle Entertainment) had to be sold in order to avoid an antitrust problem. I knew that the other major casino companies could do a bunch of business there. I had to separate myself from them, and fast. What did I do? I was in the middle of buying another casino, but I killed that deal and immediately got on my plane and flew to Vegas to meet with then CEO of Pinnacle, Anthony Sanfilippo. I offered him a $50 million deposit—completely nonrefundable. I told Anthony that if I didn't close on this deal, he could take the money I put up and sell the casino to someone else.

The building was barely out of the ground, I knew I needed at least $800 million to complete the project, and I had to get the deal approved by the gaming board—all of these could have impacted my ability to close. But I knew that this might have been my only chance to get into the Lake Charles gaming market, and I was ready. Having the ability to put up $50 million and make a big bet on myself and my company is what it took to get the deal done.

Everybody blinked when I staked that amount of money! But I was in a position to do that because I had accumulated the necessary cash.

The same thing happened when I put up $100 million nonrefundable to buy the Houston Rockets, fully aware at the time that I might not be able to obtain the necessary financing. Because I never stopped thinking ahead in building up cash, I was able to fulfill the lifelong dream of buying a sports franchise in my hometown.

LISTEN!

Okay, so you're not in position (yet!) to make those sorts of deals, but the same principle applies to any sort of business. Want to know an easy rule to make certain you always have adequate cash on hand? Never put your lifestyle ahead of the growth of your business.

I've seen it for years. All of a sudden, young companies start making an extra $20,000 a month, and instead of using it to help their businesses grow, the owners buy new homes and new cars. Then their business slips a little, and they end up working like hell, trying to keep up their personal lifestyle.

In fairness, I also own a nice home, boats, and planes. But those purchases never occurred before making certain that all my businesses had sufficient cash to leverage opportunities at all times. I've always kept the majority of my money in my company. I bitch to everyone that I never have money because I keep it all in the business!

But that's why I've gone from $4 million to $4 billion in thirty years—I didn't go out and buy $100 million Picassos like some people. I didn't buy a house in Malibu. I used that money to buy more companies and to build buildings.

About five or six years ago, I took a big dividend out of the company—roughly $600 million in cash. I didn't go buy a new plane. I didn't go buy a new boat. I didn't go buy a piece of art. I sat there with the money, knowing that times were going to get tough. I was able to make some huge acquisitions. That's because I was liquid when there was a downturn.

"Never put your lifestyle ahead of
the growth of your business."

This comes back to something I say a lot, but it bears repeating: when things are good, we tend to forget that things can get bad. One of the biggest mistakes an entrepreneur can make is to assume the good times will always last. I've been through three major economic downturns, and being prepared is the only way to weather these storms. During the 2008 recession, my company wasn't caught off guard. Our income dropped 10 percent. Fortunately, we survived by being ready in advance. We always have cash or credit capacity set aside, ready for the next downturn. And so should you.

Next, address the issue of bank financing. The first step is simple: get it before you need it. I cannot stress this enough. Work to obtain bank financing as soon as you can get it, which is generally easier to secure when the economy is strong and your business is doing well. Not only does that give you the best chance to get financing on the best possible terms, but when things take a downturn—which they inevitably will—you're going to have cash within reach to make it through.

Additionally, pursuing bank financing when your business is doing well lets you leverage those factors that every lender looks for—positive cash flow, and solid and consistent revenue and profits, among other things.

Pay attention to your personal credit, especially if your business is new, with little or no credit activity. The biggest factor in many banks' decisions to lend businesses money is the owners' personal credit rating. To boost your credit score, be sure to pay personal bills on time and keep a low ratio of debt to available credit on personal credit cards and credit lines.

LISTEN!

Don't just go into the bank and tell them you need money. Walk in there like you know how to borrow money and have a thorough business plan with you. Be sure to have a comprehensive overview of your current circumstances, specifically why you're asking for the money, as well as a strategy that outlines your future plans. And don't make the mistake of limiting your plan's outlook to the next thirty days. Instead, map out plans for the next one to three years—the longer and more detailed, the more favorably a lender will view your application.

But as I like to say, don't go so far as to start drinking your own Kool-Aid. If, by chance, the scenario you lay out to a lender is too good to be sustainable, you're going to be out of business even if you obtain the cash you're after. That's because you won't be able to meet that aggressive a level of obligation—meaning that you can't afford the loan.

Here's what I do and what I suggest you do as well. With every scenario and every deal, I run a best-case scenario, a likely scenario, and a worst-case scenario. If you do that—and provided your numbers work—feel free to offer the banker your best-case scenario.

However, this strategy comes with a few cautions. First and foremost, don't lie to yourself. If the numbers say you can't manage your best-case scenario, don't talk yourself into it, no matter how much you may need the money. Be absolutely certain your best-case scenario is, in fact, doable. Otherwise, you're driving your business straight off a cliff.

Additionally, don't overlook the value of drawing up a worst-case scenario. That's because you want to be confident that you'll still be in business if anything and everything goes wrong. In the worst situation possible, where will you be? Everyone wants to assume that everything is going to work out, but know what numbers you'll be looking at in the event that things turn out badly. What will you do when you have half the amount of business you thought you were going to have?

It's perfectly fine to keep your worst-case scenario to yourself. After all, you want the money. But along the way, don't lie to yourself (or the bank) and convince yourself that a certain plan is going to work out when the numbers say otherwise. Why? Because, sooner or later, the worst is going to happen, and you need to understand whether you're going to be able to survive or not. Eighty percent of the time, you're going to hit the worst-case scenario and not the best-case scenario, so make sure your business is still going to be in business under the worst-case scenario.

If you're turned down for a loan or line of credit, don't give up. If you don't already have one, get a business credit card. Not only can that offer some source of necessary funds, but using it responsibly will help build your business's credit rating and history, which, in turn, may help if you try again to obtain bank financing.

No matter the specifics, remember that working capital is everything. A business without a ready source of cash is playing with fire, day in and day out.

That was my concern with Nicole Di Rocco of NICOLITA Swimwear, a company featured on *Billion Dollar Buyer*. The maker of unique swimwear once had a contract to supply a department store, only to have it fall apart after the store renegotiated her contract for a net 90 arrangement. Translated: ninety days to be paid by a buyer. Meanwhile, she lacked sufficient capital to bridge the gap.

Happily, when I met Nicole, she readily acknowledged her need for working capital with which to grow her business. Over my time working with her, she was able to significantly expand her company's line of credit to carry her through the ninety-day waiting period to get paid. It also paid off for her: she accepted a deal with me worth $175,000 for swimwear for use in my resorts as well as for retail sale. All because she quickly realized that, when it comes to growing a small business, working capital is everything.

TILMAN'S TARGETS

- Working capital is the lifeblood of any business.
- Loans and lines of credit are two excellent sources of ready cash.

- Borrow money when times are good, even if you don't need it.
- Draw up a worst-case scenario that you can keep to yourself. If everything goes wrong, you want to be certain you can stay in business.

CHAPTER 5

THE PITFALLS OF PROPERTY LEASES

E very entrepreneur who starts a business is focused (or should be focused) on the usual things—product, production and labor costs, and marketing, among many others.

Those are all perfectly valid concerns. But one other issue tends to fly under the radar of many entrepreneurs' attention: property leases.

At first glance, that may seem like a relatively minor concern. After all, property is nothing more than a place to conduct business. If you have a place that suits your purposes, what else is there to worry about?

A lot.

This goes back to an issue I raised in the prior chapter. When planning for the future, it's natural for entrepreneurs to map out plans they fully expect to run like clockwork—a complete and unqualified success. Most likely, no entrepreneur in the history of business has ever started something without utter confidence that the venture would move forward and flourish.

But it's equally valuable to draw up a plan B of sorts—one that turns out significantly less successful. Again, that's something you should feel free to keep to yourself, though it's essential to anticipate what things will be like if, by chance, your business struggles or, even worse, fails to survive.

That's where property leases can come into play, and not necessarily in a good way. If your business does struggle or go under completely, and you decide to give up (in my view, something that many businesses do way too early, but we'll get to that later), what happens to the property you were leasing for the business?

If you haven't been proactive, you keep on paying. That's what can happen.

Think about that for a moment. You may be paying a relatively small amount to lease property—say $5,000 a month—on a five-year lease. If things go bad and you're forced to close, everything comes to a sudden halt—except for your lease payments. If you've been in business for two years and shut down, that's $5,000 a month for the next three years—$180,000—that you may have to keep paying, even though your business is long gone, all because the landlord hasn't found a replacement tenant.

What many entrepreneurs fail to realize is that leases can be comparable to taking out a bank loan. Regardless of what happens, you owe that money, and the bank—or in this case, the landlord—is going to make certain you pay it.

If you try to refuse to pay what you owe, watch out. Like

any lender, your landlord can bring a suit against you and garnish any assets you have. They have every right to collect what's owed them, like anyone who loans you money. Signing a lease is exactly like signing a promissory note. When you put your name on the lease, you're guaranteeing that you'll pay what's owed on that lease.

It goes without saying that this situation can cripple you financially for years to come. For instance, if you shut down your business at an outside location and try to keep it going in your home or garage, you're still burdened by a lease payment for space you no longer use. Thinking about giving up on the old business and starting something completely new? Again, you're going to have to do it with a financial burden hanging over your head—often a very significant one.

LISTEN!

Fortunately, the situation doesn't have to turn out that way, but you need to know a few strategies before you sign on the dotted line. First, try negotiating a clause that allows you to cancel your lease if revenue projections haven't reached a certain goal by the six-month or one-year anniversary of the lease.

Another choice is a buyout clause. This gives you the option of paying to terminate your lease if your business isn't generating sufficient revenue to afford the expense. The downside is that a buyout clause can be expensive, maybe as much as fifty cents on the dollar of the amount owed for the remainder of the lease.

> This can depend on prevailing market conditions and how confident the landlord is about finding a new lessee to take your place.

As another form of protection, pay attention to the length of the lease. First, if you're just starting out with a relatively new business, a long lease can be a bad idea—the longer the lease, the longer your liability if your business doesn't succeed. The general rule of thumb in terms of shielding your liability is the shorter, the better.

Of course, a landlord may not be particularly enthusiastic about a short lease. He or she wants as much security as possible, so any tenant is locked in for the longest time possible.

This can be addressed by a lease with term options. For instance, you agree to an initial two-year lease with more options to renew when that time period ends—for example, options of two or three additional years. While that gives both you and your landlord additional flexibility, understand that the landlord will likely insist that any additional options will mean an increase in the rent you pay every month.

If you're looking at term options, negotiate them in your favor. For example, make it clear in your lease agreement that you're the one who has the right to exercise the additional term options, meaning that your landlord has to agree, as long as you stick to the requirements outlined in the lease terms.

Another strategy is making certain you have the option of finding someone else to sublease the property if you can't make a go of it. In this situation, somebody else effectively takes over your lease, freeing you from further financial responsibility. To avoid problems, ensure your lease says your landlord can't unreasonably refuse to consent to a new tenant who's financially qualified.

Of course, this is all part of doing your due diligence before signing a lease. Get a sense of the rent on comparable properties, to make sure your financial commitment is in line. Understand all the costs tacked on to the lease payment itself. Review any stated increases in lease payments, as well as your obligation for utilities and other expenses.

Lastly, it's never a bad idea to work with an experienced real estate attorney to address these and other issues. That can make your lease a valuable component of your business rather than a needless liability.

TILMAN'S TARGETS

- Make certain you understand how to get out of a lease early, including buyout provisions, subleasing, and other options.
- In general, look for a short-term lease—ideally, with renewal options that you can choose to exercise.
- Know all costs associated with a lease.
- Work with an attorney experienced in commercial real estate to help negotiate the best possible lease package.

CHAPTER 6
KNOW YOUR NUMBERS

As you can tell from my show *Billion Dollar Buyer*, as well as the ideas and topics covered in this book, there's a great deal that I like about working with entrepreneurs. They have vision. They have courage. They have commitment to their ideas and their products. And they have the nerve to keep going when many others would happily throw in the towel.

But some things do bother me. And nothing bothers me more than an entrepreneur who doesn't know his or her numbers.

It bothers me a hell of a lot.

By numbers, I mean everything to do with your business. Cost of supplies. Cost of production. Labor costs. Costs of sales. Margins. I won't bother going into any explanation regarding them. You should know exactly what I'm talking about. And if you don't, you'd better find out.

"Know your numbers. Numbers don't lie."

As an entrepreneur, chances are excellent that you know—or certainly should know—all those numbers are essential to understand. But in my dealing with entrepreneurs of all sorts, I'm constantly amazed at how many entrepreneurs don't know these numbers like the backs of their hands.

First off, numbers concerning your business are the lifeblood of that enterprise. They tell you everything you need to know about where your business has been, where it is now, and, perhaps most importantly, where it's headed. They offer the single most valuable and accurate read of your business in its entirety.

That's a hell of a lot that goes without the attention it needs, if you don't know your numbers.

Just as bad, even entrepreneurs who have a basic understanding of their numbers often don't know those numbers at the level of detail they should. From where I stand, an entrepreneur needs to know numbers down to their decimal points. For instance, they should know if their utility costs are truly 4 percent. If you know your costs to every tenth, at the end of the month, you can see where you need to fix those numbers.

That kind of specific knowledge arms you with the best information to confidently make good decisions, particularly the tough ones.

I make it an ongoing, everyday point to ensure I'm completely familiar with all the numbers having to do with my businesses.

I also make budgets an everyday priority. I have both weekly and monthly budgets to keep track of what we're doing, from a profitability standpoint. I even run daily reports, which I call my "flash reports," for each of my different businesses. These flash reports show me the most important information that allows me to know where I stand at all times. Knowing how your business is performing from a financial standpoint on a daily basis is equally important as selling your product.

You can and should do the same. Know what your lease payment is for the month, what your salaries are, cost of sales, and other known operating expenses, and track all of those expenses regularly, along with your revenue. To the extent that your revenue is greater than your expenses, then you know if you're making money and if you're on budget or not. Simple, but a key part of my success.

You don't want to be surprised thirty or forty-five days after the end of a month to suddenly realize that you lost money. You need to know exactly where you are within a 5 to 10 percent degree of certainty—all the time.

Knowing your numbers is essential, no matter how your business is performing—the more specific that knowledge, the better. If your business is on the upswing, you must know everything about the income and expenses, to the smallest detail. If you don't have a solid handle on the numbers for inventory, overhead, staffing, and supplies, you're going to find it that much harder to take your business to the next level. Your decisions won't be as sound, you won't be able to think on your feet and make good decisions quickly, and you may inadvertently pass on great opportunities, because you don't know if your numbers can handle them or not.

Numbers are just as vital when your business is struggling. Lacking specific knowledge, you may be unable to identify the problems holding back your business. Worse, you may decide that one particular area of your business is the culprit, only to discover later that your lack of knowledge about your numbers led you to something that wasn't the problem at all.

When do you make that discovery? All too often, when you hand the keys to your landlord shortly after you shut down your business.

Knowing your numbers inside and out doesn't stop with the numbers themselves. It's also essential that you put them in perspective, so you know whether your numbers are where they should be.

I mentioned this in the prior chapter, when I discussed obtaining the most favorable lease possible. It's critical to know what the going rate is for a certain amount of space—that is, what's a good deal? Are there areas in the town or city your business is located where you're going to pay a premium for space?

The same goes for your other numbers. Know that your labor costs should be in a certain range. Utilities should never account for more than a specified amount. These and other frameworks let you see a broader picture of what parts of your business are on solid ground and where you need to make some serious adjustments.

Knowing your numbers is also a critical element of your sales pitch, regardless of who you may be pitching. If you're talking with a banker or some other lender, you'd better know your numbers inside and out. And if you're talking with a potential business partner—such as me—your knowledge of your numbers should be every bit as thorough.

Still, when I'm talking with budding entrepreneurs, the conversation goes the same way all too often:

"What's your cost of labor?" I ask.

"Uh . . ."

"How many employees do you have now?"

"Eleven."

"Can those eleven employees take you from $2 million to $4 million in sales?"

"Well . . ."

"You do understand that if they can do that, you've effectively cut your labor costs in half, right?"

"Um, sure . . ."

And on it goes. Are margins holding up, including gross margins and net margins? Are you turning over more money but only making slightly more or the same in revenue? Sometimes the answers come from confusion rather than out of ignorance, such as mixing up labor costs with lease costs or mistakenly combining the two.

No matter the specifics, I'm continually shocked about how little people know regarding the economics of their own company. In fact, when I go in and meet these new companies, I can tell within three minutes if they have any idea what they're doing.

All this raises a question: If I can tell in a couple of minutes whether a business's numbers look good or not, what am I looking at?

I start with revenue. Next is cost of sales. After that are labor and other expenses. There are other issues to bear in mind, but those are the primary ones.

When it comes to numbers, most entrepreneurs assume that to make more money you have to boost revenue. That's true, but not always. For instance, a business with labor expenses at 25 percent immediately becomes more profitable if those costs go down (a theme I talk about all the time on *Billion Dollar Buyer*). Selling more may mean nothing if your costs continue to increase—something that knowledge of your numbers helps you keep under control.

Although this sort of knowledge and analysis—being able to really dig into your numbers—is critical to boosting your business and pushing it to the next level, this doesn't mean all entrepreneurs need to be numbers whizzes. If you're trying to run a company but can't keep track of costs and sales, make it a top priority to hire people who can.

They'd better be strong, because without them, you're not going to survive. That's because your numbers mean everything. Treat them that way.

TILMAN'S TARGETS

- Knowing your numbers is the most essential part of being able to take your business to the next level.
- Make daily flash reports and budgets a priority.

- A complete knowledge of numbers is also critical to any sort of successful sales pitch.
- If you don't or can't master your numbers, partner with or hire someone who can.

SECTION 3

THE 95:5 RULE: WHAT'S YOUR "FIVE"?

Being in business can involve all sorts of formulas. But when it comes to what can make your business either a success or an ongoing struggle, I always use a simple ratio to make sure I'm paying attention to what really matters.

LISTEN!

I call it the 95:5 rule. The breakdown is simple. Most moderately successful businesses are good at about 95 percent of what they do. It's the remaining 5 percent that can determine whether the business excels or not.

I've seen businesses wrestle with this over and over. Often, they haven't identified that critical 5 percent. Sometimes, they're needlessly worried about the 95 percent that *is* working. Other times they know the 5 percent that isn't working but don't know what they can do to change that. Maybe they refuse to believe that particular 5 percent is all that important.

That 5 percent isn't just important—it's absolutely essential. And that 5 percent can appear in all sorts of ways.

Five percent may not seem like much, but it is. The chapters in this section show you how to know your 5 percent and what you can do to make your business excel.

CHAPTER 7

GET TO KNOW
YOUR "FIVE"

On the surface, the 95:5 ratio may seem completely out of balance.

I've heard it from all sorts of entrepreneurs: How can a measly 5 percent help or hurt my business so much? How can such a small part matter, especially when most everything else is working so well?

Believe me, it can.

Let's break down what we're discussing. By the 95 percent, I'm talking about the portion of your business that functions well. It can refer to the core competence of your business, be that food service, landscaping, or any other activity.

For instance, in the case of my network of restaurants, the 95 percent refers to the consistent quality of the food, the cleanliness of the facilities, and the performance of the restaurant staff—in other words, the basics. I know that our staff is properly trained, our menus are up to date and accurate, and point-of-sale systems and other types of technology are functioning as they should be. That's our 95 percent, because all the necessary systems and procedures are in place.

The 5 percent is the real difference driver, the tipping point that, when addressed properly and consistently, moves our restaurants past that 95-percent level.

Unfortunately, that critical 5 percent can suffer in all sorts of ways:

- A server brings a drink without a napkin. (This drives me nuts every single time I see it.)
- A four-person table has one chair that doesn't match the other three.
- A perfectly prepared meal is served on the wrong type of plate.
- Overhead fans turn at different rates of speed.
- Trash and cigarette butts litter the parking lot.

But the 5 percent doesn't always have to be a negative:

- It can mean knowing the names of repeat customers.
- It can mean knowing where a particular customer prefers to sit.
- It can mean knowing whether certain customers

appreciate frequent check-ins while they're eating or prefer to be left alone.

- It can mean escorting a customer to the restroom if he or she doesn't know where it is.

Those and other things are what I mean by that 5 percent, those elements that, when executed well, can set your business apart and help propel it to the next level—or, at the same time, hinder your growth if they're not done right or ignored altogether.

These and other examples show how hard it can be to identify the 5 percent. When a business is struggling to grow, it's understandable if the owner looks for the most obvious issues—lack of cash flow, for instance, or production headaches.

But there are issues beyond the obvious. Stories have been written about me saying that I can see a burned-out light bulb forty thousand feet in the sky. Why is that? Because when I go into my businesses, I pay attention and look for what's wrong. I've trained myself to see little things that matter. It drives some of my colleagues crazy, but I take their complaints as compliments. Little things truly matter in taking a business from good to extraordinary.

Sometimes the 5-percent problem is something the business has done for years. Maybe it's the way they market themselves, maybe it's production costs that have been unnecessarily high, or maybe it's some other strategy or practice they're using because, well, that's the way they've always done it. In a business with a long-running 5 percent that's a matter of habit, it's often a testimony to the product's strength that the business has managed to stay alive! Five-percent problems that float under the radar can be that serious.

Sometimes the 5 percent is an issue that an entrepreneur or business owner knows is there. The problem is they don't know what to do about it. Maybe they say, "We know our costs are too high, but we don't know where else to look for production supplies." Other times, the problem is obvious but of such a personal nature that any action to correct it may seem more damaging than the problem itself—think of the punch line to the joke about the business owner who knows he should fire his idiot son: "But I have to sleep with his mother."

Sometimes the 5 percent stems from complacency—an attitude that 95 percent is good enough. Well, it may be good enough, but that 5 percent you choose to ignore can mean the difference between business as usual and a business that truly excels—a business that blossoms into a regional or national player versus one that's small and bound to remain that way.

I park my car, and I'm walking into a restaurant. I see a smashed Coke can or a broken beer bottle. As I near the entrance, I notice some dead plants with cigarette butts and candy wrappers nearby. I reach for the front door. The glass has smudges on it because the hostess isn't wiping it down constantly.

Those observations take a minute or two at the most. But I know what that restaurant experience will be like before I even walk in the front door. I can tell you right then and there whether I am going to have sharp service, sharp food, sharp everything. And I'm barely through the front door.

That's the 5 percent I'm talking about.

LISTEN!

A culture of always being on the lookout for the 5 percent is something that I've built in each and every one of my businesses. I urge you to do the same. You should aim for a culture that puts the 5 percent at the forefront of your thoughts, decisions, and actions. Don't be shy or bashful about letting others know just how critical that is.

This culture must permeate your business. Show the people with whom you work that the 95 percent smoothly humming along isn't what truly matters when it comes to separating yourself from everyone else—it's the 5 percent. You're always watching for the 5 percent, and they should be as well. Five percent is the attention to potentially small details that a great business owner and staff might miss but a great team would rarely overlook.

Have them proactively work at the 5 percent. If you run a restaurant, tell your servers to keep an eye on their customers' plates. If somebody hasn't eaten their food, notify a manager, who can visit the table and ask, "I noticed you didn't eat your food—is everything okay?" That's because dissatisfied customers often won't say anything. It's up to you to take the first step to check to see if there's an issue that needs to be resolved.

The same goes for any business. If a customer buys an expensive product, follow up by phone. Ask questions like, "Is everything okay? Is the product everything you wanted it to be?" There may or may not be a problem. But a little effort on your part shows that their business matters to you, and you're ready to address any issues that may arise.

One way I view it is in terms of a thermostat in a room. If a room is too hot or too cold, you adjust the thermostat by just a degree, maybe two, and it will change the room's comfort level.

Apply that concept to your business. If you make just a 1 percent improvement in the 5 percent that needs attention, think about the results you can achieve—like the room that becomes comfortable because of the slightest temperature adjustment. So, too, with your business—a seemingly small change can have a big impact.

Additionally, consider how that 1 or 2 percent difference can help separate you from your competitors.

Approach the situation from a numbers perspective—a 1 or 2 percent difference for the better in your business may not seem like much, but it can translate into significant extra revenue that you can earmark to expand your business or help acquire a competitor.

It's also essential to remember that, unlike the "paddle" I discussed in the introduction, you have complete control over that 5 percent. The weather or a power outage is out of your hands, but that important 5 percent is something you can wake up to every day and address.

This approach is subtle but powerful. You're not necessarily looking at some sort of major change or upheaval. After all, if you boost the thermostat in the room by ten degrees, you're not going to be comfortable. More likely, you're going to be boiling! By the same token, dropping it by ten degrees can leave you shivering. Either way, it's completely ineffective and counterproductive.

The same holds true for your business. Taking your business to that next level by addressing the 5 percent is handling the factors that can set you apart. If you consider a drastic change or solution, you may inadvertently affect part of the 95 percent that you already do well. In other words, you're fixing something that isn't broken.

There are lots of examples of businesses with great products that don't grow into all they can be because of not paying attention to the 5 percent. For instance, a lot of talented, creative people go into business, only to have their business side emerge as the 5 percent that ultimately causes them to struggle. (Later in this section I'll discuss the importance of balancing strengths when choosing partners and coworkers. That's a key strategy for anyone creative, or anyone with a particular strength or ability: to find someone who complements their skills instead of duplicating them.)

As I mentioned earlier, the 5 percent that hurts a business can come from seemingly small, insignificant things. For instance, a mailer that reads "at the corner of Oak and Frost" instead of "225 Frost Boulevard." Or a food package with one small misspelling in its instructions.

Take it as a compliment that you have the ability to see a burned-out light bulb at forty thousand feet away. That means you notice seemingly insignificant things that others might miss but that can completely cripple a business. If you're the kind of entrepreneur who has a knack for spotting the small stuff, keep it up. If you're not, make sure you partner with someone who can. Either way, always watch the details.

How else can you stay on top of the 5 percent?

LISTEN!

Listen to your partner, customers, suppliers, and anyone else with an opinion about your business. Ask them, "If you could change one thing about what my business does, what might that one thing be?" Also, pay attention to online reviews and feedback.

Never lose sight of your customer's perspective. Here's what I mean by that. A restaurant manager arrives at the restaurant before it's dark, goes inside, and stays there. Perfectly fine, but this doesn't let him see what customers see when they pull into the parking lot after sundown. Maybe a sign isn't turned on. Maybe trash has accumulated, or someone has dumped out a car ashtray right in the middle of a parking space.

The point is, you can't forget to experience your business like a customer does. That's why I urge all my restaurant managers to get their butts outside and walk the property. Seeing what a customer sees can boost your hold on that critical 5 percent.

Obviously, not every business allows you to walk the property. But try to walk in their shoes whenever possible. Ask them point-blank how they were treated at your business. What did they notice? Was it something that boosted your business in their eyes, or diminished it?

Never become complacent. No matter if your business is soaring or struggling, never take a break from looking at that all-important 5 percent. Because when it comes to working to achieve that breakout every business wants, the 95 percent that's working just fine tends to take care of itself. The 5 percent that isn't working might end up taking care of you, and not in the way anyone wants.

TILMAN'S TARGETS

- The 95:5 rule—95 percent of your business may be operating fine, but seek out the 5 percent that's wrong.
- Don't get complacent: always look for the 5 percent.
- View your business through your customer's eyes.
- The 5 percent that harms your business can be made up of small things.

CHAPTER 8
KNOW AND LEVERAGE YOUR STRENGTHS

Many business advisors—and others as well—urge people to work on building up their weaknesses. The thinking is, by getting better at what you don't do especially well, you become a better-rounded, more capable person.

I don't disagree with that. We should all work to improve the things we're not good at. For me, that would be a very long list, and yours probably would be too.

But don't forget to leverage your strengths at the same time.

I like to say we all know what we know and what we don't know. We may not want to admit it, but the truth about ourselves is usually clear. Deep down, we recognize what our strengths are, in addition to those skills that don't match up with our abilities.

That kind of honesty is important if you're an entrepreneur—or anyone else, for that matter. In fact, one of the biggest mistakes people make is being unable to admit what they don't know.

I've seen it for years and, more recently, on *Billion Dollar Buyer*. I've met with entrepreneurs and businesspeople who are absolutely convinced they're good at something they're not all that good at. Some may think they're good at marketing, while others are certain they understand the need for ongoing cash flow to help their business grow. Many have convinced themselves they know everything about how to scale up their businesses.

One of the things that has always come naturally to me is my ability to recognize what I'm good at and what I'm not good at. As I've sometimes said, I have to think about how to put gas in my car. Change the oil? I'd take lashes instead of trying to do that.

A guy can take an engine apart and put it back together, but most don't give him any respect for being able to do it. But he's the smartest guy in the world to me. The painter who can paint a perfect line? My line would be here and there and all over the place.

"I can look at a business and its numbers and within a few minutes know if that business has the stuff to become really successful. It's what I'm good at, and I know this."

That's why I urge every entrepreneur to be brutally honest with himself or herself. It's critical to know what skills you bring to the table and those you lack. Without that honesty, you may not be able to grow a business in all aspects and to keep that growth going through a balance of skills (more about this in the next chapter).

People—especially younger entrepreneurs—constantly ask me if I think they need to go back to school to get an MBA. My answer is always the same—if you need that, you'll know it. You'll know if business comes naturally to you or if you need more formal education to fill in some of the cracks. And for many people, getting an MBA is a way to increase their overall skill level and, from there, apply that to moving their business to the next level.

Going back to school doesn't automatically mean an MBA. In an episode of *Billion Dollar Buyer*, Kismet Cosmetics founder Caitlin Picou worked with the entrepreneurial school at the University of Houston to build and refine an effective business plan. You can certainly do the same, as there are many online and onsite business programs throughout the country where entrepreneurs can become much better versed in the workings and strategies of the business, without any prohibitive time commitments.

But going back for more schooling isn't just an opportunity to shore up business skills you may lack. It's also a way to sharpen those things you're already good at.

That ties back to the central idea of this chapter—improve at what you're not particularly good at, and lean and build on those strengths you know you have. If you know you have the gift of creativity, leverage that for all it's worth. On the other hand, if you're good at numbers, for instance, rely on that ability.

Sometimes, a strength may not even be a particular business

skill. For example, one thing I urge every entrepreneur to do is to never give up. Don't admit defeat until they come and padlock your front door. Call that stubbornness, call it confidence, but it's certainly a strength. If you can ignore the naysayers, everyone around you who says you can't possibly make it, that's a strength to rely on.

Occasionally, you meet an entrepreneur who's not certain what his or her strengths are. Maybe they're too modest to point out a personal strength. Or maybe they're the opposite—"I'm so good at everything, I can't pick just one!"

Here's where a little feedback can be helpful. Ask your business partners what they think your particular strengths are (and, to avoid turning this into an ego party, offer to describe their strengths to them). You may hear what you expect, but you also may be pleasantly surprised, or even disappointed. Hearing this information from someone else may be just the thing you need to pinpoint those strengths you bring to the business.

LISTEN!

How you best build on your strengths depends on what those strengths are. For some, that may mean going back to school to get an MBA. For others, it can mean becoming aware of what you do well and making certain you bring that strength to your business. Don't be afraid to let others know what you have confidence in. As an example, if you're adept at analyzing numbers, and the creative guy in your group doesn't see what you see, get your points across so your business benefits from what you know best.

No matter the specifics, a business won't flourish by ignoring its strengths. It's great to become better at things you're not particularly good at, but also leverage all that you do well. After all, that's why you went into business in the first place.

TILMAN'S TARGETS

- Work on your weaknesses, but also make sure to work on your strengths.
- Ask your partners to describe what they believe to be your strengths.
- If you have a strength, build on it. Lean on it. Don't be afraid to assert your strength for the good of the business.

CHAPTER 9
PARTNER WITH COMPLEMENTARY STRENGTHS

What's a surefire formula for business failure?

Many people might answer that by saying, "Go into business with a family member or best friend."

I don't know if I agree with that entirely. Granted, there's no better way to lose a friend or a loved one than by starting a business together, only to see it flounder. But, on *Billion Dollar Buyer*, I've encountered many promising businesses that are run by friends or family members. For me, it's not so much what label goes with a particular person—friend, sibling, what have you—but what they bring to the table.

That highlights what I think matters even more. When it

comes to business success, it's far more important to partner with people who have complementary strengths.

Here's what I see all too often: you and two of your best friends have worked in a kitchen together for several years. You all know the kitchen inside and out. You decide to go into business for yourselves, as partners.

It's great that you're all strong with regard to how the kitchen operates. But it would be far better if one of you knew the kitchen, one of you knew financials, and the third friend understood the front of the house.

> "Never become partners with someone
> who has the same skill set as you."

If you think about it, that only makes sense. If you partner with people with complementary strengths, rather than the same strengths, you're covering as many of your business bases as possible. If there's an issue with the kitchen, one of the three of you has a handle on it. If obtaining fresh produce every day is becoming too expensive, the numbers person can be on top of that. The same goes for the front of the house. If reservations or scheduling is becoming backed up or confused, the friend with front-of-the-house knowledge can deal with those problems.

Unfortunately, that's not the way many entrepreneurs go about starting a business. Far too often they partner with friends without giving a moment's thought to who is good at what. You just know that you like each other, share the same dreams, and are committed to building a business you're all excited about.

There's nothing wrong with that. But if you come at this from the standpoint of strengths, you're effectively crippling your business from the very beginning. For instance, if you're both good at numbers, who's going to take the lead if you have delivery issues? Who's going to be responsible for evaluating customer feedback and addressing problems?

If everyone involved in a business has identical or even similar skills, that can lead to major headaches. But those and other issues like them prove manageable if the business leadership has different skills and strengths.

This isn't just a matter of division of responsibility. It comes back to what I discussed in the prior chapter—leveraging your strengths. Partnering with others who have different strengths and abilities allows everyone involved to play to those strengths, rather than try to scramble to address issues and challenges that don't match their skills.

Nor is "never do business with friends" a hard-and-fast rule. Anything but. One thing I emphasize is making friends in business because they're the only ones who will be there for you when you really need them.

It's also important to recognize and appreciate what strengths everyone contributes to a business. It's a mistake to assume that one person's abilities are more "important" than someone else's. As I said earlier, I admire anyone who can take apart a car's engine and put it back together. I admire someone who's able to change a car's oil quickly and efficiently! Do I look down on those skills as something less than my ability to analyze a business's numbers? Absolutely not. And if you do, not only are you dismissing the value that every skill brings to a business, but you're also degrading others' abilities.

Sometimes, when a business isn't made up of people with a range of skills, that can become obvious quickly. Maybe they have a great product with great marketing, but production and delivery are cutting off the business at the knees. That's a clear sign that someone in the mix doesn't have the skills needed to make the business perform.

Occasionally, the signs aren't all that clear-cut. Maybe a business lacking a numbers person will do well for a while, only to see costs slowly pile up and strangle cash flow.

The good news is that the thought of a business made up of people with similar abilities and strengths doesn't have to be written in stone. If you're skilled at one particular job but know that your team lacks talent in a particular area, don't be shy about bringing someone new on board who can address those holes.

That not only takes care of a skill or ability that's lacking in a business, but it also allows everyone else to do what benefits the business most: knowing their strengths and making the most of them.

I did that several years ago when I partnered with the people behind Catch, a fantastic restaurant with locations in New York and Los Angeles. What my partners Eugene Remm and Mark Birnbaum have probably done better than anybody in the industry is change with the trends and the times. They have created an environment, ambiance, atmosphere, and energy better than any other restaurant in the industry. That, and they have great food, great service, and great locations.

What they didn't have was the business expertise to fully leverage that success. They lacked the systems in place to grow, as well as the capital required to support that growth. They were ready to take that leap of faith and acknowledged they needed someone with development and growth experience, who also had the capital to steer them in the right direction.

I partnered with them 50/50—me owning 50 percent, with the remainder divided between them. Why? Because I recognized that their egos hadn't gotten in the way of them admitting they needed someone to take on these issues and challenges. They knew they needed someone like me to help take them to the promised land.

They knew what they were good at and what they weren't good at, and they didn't hesitate for a second to find someone to address the missing pieces.

In understanding that they needed to partner with someone who had different skills and insight, they showed me just how smart they were.

TILMAN'S TARGETS

- Partner with people whose skills complement your own.
- Make friends in business your personal friends.
- If you know your business lacks a certain skill set, bring in someone who can address the void.

SECTION 4
SEE THE OPPORTUNITY, SEIZE THE OPPORTUNITY

Every successful entrepreneur is, more or less, an opportunist. And I mean that in the best sense of the word.

An entrepreneur sees opportunity by building a business that's focused on something different from what others are doing. Maybe he makes an existing product better. Maybe she takes an existing product and comes up with fresh new ways to use it. No matter the specifics, every entrepreneur looks to build a business that capitalizes on the opportunity he or she can see.

But some entrepreneurs go beyond that. For one thing, many entrepreneurs capture opportunity in circumstances that, to almost everyone else, don't seem to be much of an opportunity at all. As I'll share in the next chapter, I'm one of the entrepreneurs who was fortunate enough—and opportunistic enough—to make the most of a situation riddled with chaos and confusion.

Then there's another kind of entrepreneur, one who recognizes that even the greatest ideas and business concepts aren't necessarily overnight successes. They see that some businesses will take time to grow and prosper, and that it will be up to them to have the confidence and conviction to stand by their vision.

They're what I refer to as the "not yet" entrepreneurs. What they see is no less real than immediate success, but success that's going to take time to happen.

That offers all of us a lesson in persistence, one characterized by patience, commitment, and, perhaps most important, the understanding that success takes time and perspective. They're as confident as the most impatient entrepreneur that success is on the way.

Just not now.

CHAPTER 10
A FIVE-YEAR REPRIEVE

If you want to talk about being an opportunist—about making the most of a situation where it seemed as though no opportunity was anywhere in sight—let me take you back to the 1980s in Houston, Texas.

When I was in my late twenties, about the time I was experiencing some business success, there were hundreds of banks across Houston. In many ways, it was a buyer's market for companies in need of financing. With so many institutions competing against one another for business, it was a great time for entrepreneurs to look for funding and other means of financial assistance to start or grow a company. Banks and lenders were fighting tooth and nail for every bit of business they could land.

Going back a bit further to the 1970s, Texas had the most banks of any state in America. Not only was the oil business going great guns, local legislators had limited outside competition by prohibiting any lender outside the state from doing business here. That made for a closed, competitive market.

But it didn't last. After embargoes were removed in the 1980s, the price of oil plummeted. Eager to pick up the slack, banks began shifting their attention away from the oil industry and into the commercial real estate market. But after incentives were eliminated in real estate, that portion of banks' portfolios also began to fall apart.

The aftershocks were enormous. From 1980 to 1989, 425 Texas commercial banks failed. That included nine of the ten biggest ones. In 1988 alone, 175 Texas banks went under—representing $47.3 billion, about 25 percent of the entire state's banking assets.

You had banks collapsing across the board. Every savings and loan failed. Every Tuesday the FDIC would come in and close three or four more banks in town. You could almost set your watch to it.

This went on for two years.

It was horrific to watch, and it also resulted in an enormous shift in the banking industry, which was boiled down and consolidated. That's why you have banks today with trillions of dollars in assets, which are too big to fail because the government came in and helped them take over other banks. They're basically rollups of all the banks that existed back then.

When all was said and done, after the world basically fell apart, every bank in Houston had failed except five or six. And, as I said earlier, every savings and loan failed.

I didn't realize at the time how much I would learn from the experience—as useful a lesson as I have ever received. In my case, I had loans at eight to nine different banks, totaling about $2 million. Like a lot of other people, I scrambled and made deals whenever and however I could. I kept fighting and fighting. I worked out interest-only deals at a few banks and consolidated loans at others. It was a never-ending juggling act. I was trying to stay alive, and some days the prognosis didn't look especially good.

In fact, one time I switched watches with my lawyer Steve Scheinthal in the elevator on the way up to talk with bankers. I thought it better that the guy asking for a deal was wearing a little Seiko watch instead of some fancy gold Rolex!

But, in its own way, the situation worked out. Simply put, every bank with which I was doing business failed. As a result, I didn't have to make any debt payments—there was no one to make payments to.

As it turned out, the bureaucracy and mechanics of banking and government worked in my favor. Given all the time and energy required to shut down all the banks and reallocate all the funds, it took them five years to get to me! They had bigger issues to worry about.

That gave me an invaluable five-year reprieve during which I had a lot more cash to work with, since I wasn't making loan payments. And in that five-year period, I built Landry's locations in Galveston, Corpus Christi, San Antonio, Kemah, and Dallas.

Not a bad run of success when everything else seemed to be going straight to hell. And the fact that I had cash-flow businesses ensured my growth, while others operating on an accounts-receivable basis (where you wait to be paid) were struggling.

Even though that five-year window of opportunity gave me the chance to go on a roll, that's not to say it was easy. Finding funds to pay for the kind of expansion I wanted to pursue was incredibly difficult. I used credit cards, cash, equipment leases, and most anything else I could get my hands on. I couldn't go to any banks because there were essentially no banks to go to. Whatever money I found to fund my business, I had to piece it together on my own. Since funding had been readily available not long before, the scramble to track down what I needed was both exciting and scary—exciting because I had spotted opportunity and was trying to make the most of it, and scary because leveraging that opportunity involved a whole new playing field.

Of course, my five-year break didn't last forever. The FDIC did eventually get around to me. Still, it was a great deal. In 1991, they agreed to waive all interest charges on what I owed. I wrote them a check for $2 million, and that was that. It was interest-free money for five years.

Naturally, this entire situation involved a fair degree of luck on my part. Since the government had much bigger players than me to focus on, I was lucky they took as long as they did to address my situation. I wasn't big enough to be at the front of the line.

But this story is also a great illustration of recognizing opportunity and making the most of it. Since the financial world was going to hell, it would've been understandable to panic, assume that finances would never be the same as they once were, and throw in the towel. You could see evidence of that everywhere. Apartment buildings were being left only partially built. Office buildings remained vacant. Residential projects had roads put in, but no houses constructed. It was scary and depressing, and it would have been simple to give up—especially if you wanted to grow like I wanted to. But there were hardly any banks to approach.

I didn't throw in the towel. One reason was a truth that I had come to learn and that I've never forgotten.

LISTEN!

When things are bad, we often tend to forget that they're going to be good again. Further, when things are good, we forget that they're going to be bad again. You need to prepare for both types of situations, because they're both headed your way, sooner or later.

Granted, this was an extreme environment in which it was definitely hard to keep the faith. If nothing else, having watched hundreds of banks go out of business, and seeing businesses of all sorts collapse as a result, it wasn't easy to keep watching and waiting for things to get better. Fortunately, I was able to do so.

Again, having cash-flow businesses where customers pay on the spot—order a meal, pay for it—helped me when the economy struggled. In fact, every time there was a hiccup in the economy, I grew because I had the cash on hand to capitalize when my competitors didn't. If yours is a cash-flow operation, you can do the same—just make certain to accumulate as much cash as possible when conditions are good.

If yours isn't a cash-flow operation, you may not find out things are bad until thirty, sixty, or ninety days after you sent your last invoice, so you need to make even more of an effort to accumulate cash or have a revolving line of credit in place to access cash during the bad times. Then, when all of your competitors don't have the cash to fill a big order that could save their business, you'll have access to cash to capitalize and either take that business or buy out your competitor. Like I said in an earlier chapter, when things are bad, eat the weak and grow your business—but that takes cash.

Looking back, the banking crisis was just a natural continuation of a pattern of success and struggle. Before the banking collapse took hold, people in Houston and throughout Texas were enjoying genuine boom times. Construction was thriving, and memberships at expensive country clubs soared. Expensive cars filled the streets, and private jets were ready for travel at a moment's notice.

At the time, did a lot of people forget that just as the bad times never last forever, the good times also don't go on endlessly?

I think a lot of them did. But I was determined not to fall victim to this mentality.

That's the kind of perspective that can help any entrepreneur spot opportunity, no matter the current circumstances. Regardless if things are good or bad, most of us have a tendency to assume that whatever's happening now is going to continue forever. We should know better than that, but a lot of us do it anyway.

That's why, as an entrepreneur, it's always critical to try to see the bigger picture. Perspective is everything. Never forget the ebb and flow of good times and bad. Talk to your partners, employees, advisors, customers, and others to broaden your view. What can they share to help you gain a more complete understanding of the situation? Do they see positive signs or hints of opportunity? Almost every environment, no matter how crazy or chaotic it may seem, contains opportunity for those who are willing to take a deep breath and try to see what others may be missing.

The experience with the banks also taught me another valuable lesson regarding opportunity, which I also discussed earlier, in the context of having enough working capital. Borrow money when you don't need it, because when you need it, you might not be able to borrow it. That was a lesson in opportunity that paid off handsomely further down the line.

A few years ago, I had banks throwing money at me. I decided to borrow, even though I didn't need the money at the time, and in so doing, I greatly boosted my interest costs. But all of a sudden, a large casino under construction in Lake Charles, Louisiana, became available. I was able to act faster than anybody else to acquire it, because I had the cash.

This story also illustrates that opportunity is there, no matter how big or small your business might be. During the banking crisis, I was the little fish that could be ignored for a few years, while the banking regulators took care of the bigger fish in the pond. As it happened, my size worked to my advantage.

Take that as a lesson in your own business. Even if you're

small, you can still spot great opportunities that you can leverage to build your business. In my case, I was given that opportunity because I was relatively small. And since a small business can react faster than many larger operations, you're in a better position to quickly take advantage of any opportunity you see.

LISTEN!

Always remember that the greatest opportunities are in bad times.

TILMAN'S TARGETS

- Opportunity is always there, no matter what the current conditions may be.
- When times are good, we tend to forget that at some point they're going to be bad.
- Borrow money when you don't need it, and build cash when times are good, so you can take advantage when times are bad.
- Spotting opportunity requires patience. There's always another deal.

CHAPTER 11

"I WONDER IF I'LL EVER HAVE A COMPANY THAT DOES $10 MILLION IN SALES"

Yes, that quote is from me.

I can clearly remember being twenty-two or twenty-three years old and wondering out loud if I ever would be the head of a company that had $10 million in sales.

I also remember some time later, when I was wondering about $20 million. Then $40 million. Then $100 million.

You get the picture.

In that way, I was like almost every entrepreneur alive. I dreamed about being successful and then building on that success.

If you don't have those sorts of dreams, you may not be

much of an entrepreneur. As a rule, entrepreneurs are dreamers at heart. If they weren't, they'd likely settle for making a living as an employee, just like everyone else.

But the kind of dreaming that allows entrepreneurs to spot opportunity has to be carefully managed. Maintain perspective as you dream—always look and work for something bigger and better, but understand that dreams are often made up of relatively small steps along the way.

On the other hand, dreaming that gets out of control can hinder or trip up even the most gifted and skilled entrepreneurs.

LISTEN!

Learn to be patient. Not the easiest thing for many aggressive entrepreneurs to do.

That's not to say dreaming is bad. If anything, it's essential for anyone who works to succeed. But perspective is everything.

My own story is an example of that. The current scope of my business interests is enormous, from professional sports to restaurants to gambling and entertainment.

But it's taken me thirty years to get here. And yes, I was as guilty as any entrepreneur when it comes to dreaming big. However, I also knew that building dreams has to be done systematically—with an ongoing eye to spot opportunity, but also an understanding that opportunity requires long-term commitment and patience.

I knew that from the start. I made sure that I was positioned to take full advantage of every opportunity I identified, both financially and logistically. But I never looked at any one success as the Big Dream come true, that one knockout punch in my fight to succeed. They were merely steps along the way—granted, some bigger and more significant than others, but steps nevertheless.

One significant opportunity I capitalized on occurred when I took my restaurant company public, on August 14, 1993. In the early '90s, many restaurant chains—Outback Steakhouse, The Cheesecake Factory, and others—were going public. It was a new fad among restaurants to access the public markets; everyone seemed to be doing an initial public offering (IPO). I saw that it was a great funding opportunity and did the same.

When I woke up on August 15, 1993, the day after my IPO, my personal stock in Landry's was worth over $100 million. Between 1993 and 2002, Landry's went back to the public market five more times with follow-on stock offerings and raised over $400 million to fuel our explosive growth. This is very difficult to do unless you're delivering on all your promises to investors and experiencing tremendous business success.

With all the capital that was raised, Landry's grew from approximately $30 million in revenues in 1993 to over $1 billion in revenues by 2004.

Still, I wasn't satisfied. I had this burning desire to expand Landry's business empire. Do you know how many $10.95 shrimp dinners a restaurant has to sell to pay its rent? As I told my management team, the restaurant business is one of the hardest businesses to excel at. You have to take multiple raw products that come in your back door and turn them into something you can then sell to your customers, all at a high quality and on a consistent basis. Meanwhile, retailers take the same product in and resell that same merchandise without having to do anything to it and with much less staff. And casinos, they have slot machines. There's no product to sell. Slot machines are like a bank where people make deposits, but you don't have to give them all their money back!

I had been going to Las Vegas for years with my family and knew Landry's was missing out on a tremendous opportunity if we didn't get into the casino business. So in 2004, Landry's did the largest bank and bond financing ever done on Wall Street by a restaurant company at that time and raised over $800 million. With cash in hand, we seized the opportunity to buy the Golden Nugget in Las Vegas.

Since the old ownership group had insufficient working capital, when I showed up with $340 million in hand, it was an easy decision for them to sell the Golden Nugget to me. After Landry's invested another $180 million into the casino property, the brand was resurrected, and with four more Golden Nugget Casinos and Hotels built over the next ten years, it is now one of the most recognizable names in the casino industry.

But like I say, when things are good, never forget that things can go bad. That was the case with all stocks, including restaurant and casino stocks, back in 2008 and 2009, when the financial crisis hit the United States. The share price of consumer stocks plummeted across the board, as stock multiples contracted (the price of a stock relative to its actual earnings).

Bad news for some, but an opportunity for me. Again, when things are bad, we tend to forget that things will be good again.

Since Landry's stock price had fallen to a ridiculously low number and because of my rainy-day cash and business acquaintances turned friends, I was a bull and seized the opportunity, starting in 2009, when I bought 100 percent of my company back amid fear and chaos on Wall Street. This all happened during the time General Motors and AIG, the largest insurance company in the world, went bankrupt, and investment banking giants Lehman Brothers and Bear Stearns failed. When the financial markets recovered, as I knew they would, and stock market multiples returned to normal levels, I completed my purchase in 2010. I was standing as the sole owner of Landry's, a $1.2-billion revenue company generating nearly $200 million in annual cash flow, and I had a personal net worth that qualified me for the Forbes 400 list for the first time.

That's a great story that describes an enormous jump in wealth. But it's also an example of opportunity that took more than a decade and a half to play out. And basically, it involved taking one step—the opportunity to go public—and, some sixteen years later, taking another step—the opportunity to go private again.

> "You're trying to run a marathon, and you
> haven't even shown me you can crawl."

It's like I told one entrepreneur on my show *Billion Dollar Buyer*: "I never shot for the stars. I took things one step at a time—and it took a long time." Or, as I commented to another,

"You're trying to run a marathon, and you haven't even shown me you can crawl."

In my work with entrepreneurs of all sorts, I've seen many business owners, particularly younger ones, who lose sight of that—a self-imposed impatience that can lead even the most promising business owners to want way too much, way too fast.

This circles back to the issue of humility. If you approach yourself and your business with a humble attitude, you know what you can reasonably do and what you cannot. And that allows you to take advantage of even the smallest opportunity instead of being frustrated by that One Big Break that never seems to come your way. You can position yourself to set reasonable goals.

Patience also plays into the way you approach certain deals. Many entrepreneurs make the mistake of going after business too aggressively, sending the message that they're willing to do anything to get the deal done. That can backfire in a big way. Yes, they may get the deal, but not the one they had hoped for, because the person on the other side of the table knew how badly they wanted it and pulled their pants down.

Here's what I do. Having evaluated everything I need to take into consideration, I make my best offer. I tell the person with whom I'm negotiating that it's my "walk-away offer." If that's good enough to close the deal, great. If not, I'm prepared to walk away.

The key here is to say what you mean and mean what you say. If you say you're going to walk away if the other person hesitates, make sure you do just that. That's because, more often than not, if what you offered was genuinely fair, chances are good the other person will come back to you, and the deal will get done.

Put another way, let the deal come back to you. It takes patience, it takes confidence, but it's a great way to make the most of the opportunity at hand.

It's okay to chase deals on occasion. But, just as often, take time to let the deals chase you.

LISTEN!

The lesson here is to pursue opportunity at every chance, but realistically. It has to be the right opportunity, not just any opportunity. Remember that there will always be another opportunity coming along. Don't be afraid to walk away from a deal. Don't chase a deal—let it come back to you.

Not every deal has to be a home run—singles pieced together can score just as many runs as one long ball.

TILMAN'S TARGETS

- As an entrepreneur, it's essential to dream—but to dream realistically.
- Don't chase a deal—let it come back to you.
- Not every deal has to be a home run.
- Spotting opportunity requires patience. There's always another deal on the horizon.

CHAPTER 12

DON'T EVER LOSE THE HUNGER

Watching a great athlete who rises to the occasion time and time again—a great hitter in baseball who celebrates a victory like it's the first time he's ever won anything, or a three-point shooter in basketball who never loses her enthusiasm at making a shot—makes you wonder about their motivation as you admire their athleticism.

How does he keep up that energy level? How can he keep going after championships when he already has so many under his belt?

The answer is simple: he stays hungry.

That's an invaluable lesson for everyone. Don't ever lose the hunger for what you're doing.

That may be an easy thing for many entrepreneurs to do.

Since they're just starting out, with big dreams, staying hungry is one of the last things they have to worry about.

But starting a business or trying to take an existing one to the next level can be exhausting. Physically, putting in fourteen hours a day seven days a week will wear down even the strongest among us. Add to that the emotional and psychological strain—maybe you're putting your life savings on the line, or someone else in your family is relying on your success—and it can be way too tempting to ease back occasionally, just to catch your breath.

That's perfectly okay, every now and then. But to truly make your business a success—and to continue building on that success—you must get that hunger back.

LISTEN!

Start by remembering a simple rule that I stress over and over: know what you're good at and what you're not. That's an essential component of building your business. If you know what you're good at—and make certain to work with people who have skills you don't have—you have a balance of skills to address problems and leverage opportunities at the same time.

But examine what you do well with an especially personal point of view. You're good at something. Why in the world would you not want to try to be the best you possibly can be? And why not try to be better at something than anyone else you know?

My definition of business success has to do with making money. However, success in life isn't measured in dollars or the size of your wallet.

But you can use the issue of money to your advantage. How? Feel poor. I always thought about things I couldn't afford.

What I mean by that is this: think of something you'd really like to do or own. But, you don't have the necessary cash. That's feeling poor, and it can be a powerful means of staying hungry.

Obviously, feeling poor will mean different things to different people. A young entrepreneur may feel poor because he can't buy a house. A more successful one may feel poor because she can't buy that boat she has her heart set on. No matter the dream, feeling poor can make you very, very hungry.

For me, I always had the dream of owning a sports franchise in my hometown. I was able to realize that dream with the purchase of the Houston Rockets, a deal that involved my putting up $100 million in nonrefundable cash toward a $2.2 billion price. I could have owned them years earlier for $85 million, but I couldn't come up with the money then. Even though I was very wealthy at the time, that made me feel poor, and I thought I would never have another chance, since pro franchises don't change ownership all that often. But when the Rockets became available again, I was bound to find a way to buy. Which I did.

That attitude will also keep you hungry. For me, I could have called it quits after I was worth $500 million, but my goal was to be on the Forbes billionaire list, so I didn't stop. Stay hungry because you want to be the best. The business world is sport to me, but you can't measure your success in it by wins and losses. You can measure your success only by how much money you make.

Another way to stay hungry has to do with perspective. When things are going well, it can be all too easy to kick back and become complacent. Why bust your rear if you don't need to? Let the good times roll.

If you recall my story about the banking industry in Houston in the early 1980s, you could probably picture a lot of people—bankers, businesspeople, and politicians, among others—who were absolutely convinced that the good times were there to stay. They were absolutely wrong.

Staying hungry is easier if you keep that in mind. Just because your business is growing and doing well today, don't ever make the assumption that situation is never going to change. That's because it's going to—you can be absolutely certain of that. And staying hungry when the times are good will put you in a much better position when things go sour.

You'll be able to move forward when times are challenging. If you stay hungry no matter what is happening around you, it's much easier to maintain that hunger—or ramp it up even more—when you have to struggle some. You won't have to completely shift gears.

"No matter the circumstances, be the bull."

All of this comes down to a central message: be the bull. By that I mean be strong, opportunistic, and confident, not to mention always prepared, regardless of what may be happening or is going to happen. In my case, being the bull meant following through on the purchase of the Houston Rockets by staking millions in nonrefundable cash—even though another bidder was in the lead. Teach yourself to be the same type of bull in your business.

Remember, there's a paddle for everyone's ass. And a bull is always ready to avoid the swat. For instance, in section 2, I emphasized the point of liquidity. When times are challenging and others are struggling, that makes for a bull poised to charge—a hungry bull ready to seize opportunities when others are merely scrambling to survive. Be a bull that's strong when others are weak.

But being hungry and staying hungry shouldn't be a solo effort. It's critical to surround yourself and work with others who are every bit as motivated and hungry as you. One person with passion is an asset—many people with that same level of passion are invaluable. By the same token, a passionate, hungry person working alongside others who are basically mailing it in is a surefire recipe for frustration, bitterness, and failure.

Finally, to stay hungry, never see anything as an obstacle, something impossible to overcome. Instead, take things as challenges, steps that require solutions to get to the finish line.

This addresses a problem that I'll discuss in more detail later but is worth mentioning again now. Many people throw in the towel way too early, particularly in business. They're confronted with problems—often, very significant ones—and they assume there's no way over or around them. So they give up.

I like to say that when it comes to your business, never give up until the moment they come and padlock your front door. Until then, everything and anything is possible. And if you approach things with an eye to solving challenges instead of seeing them as obstacles that can't be overcome, you'll never lose the hunger that's so critical to taking your business to the next level, and the level after that.

TILMAN'S TARGETS

- Surround yourself and work with others who are every bit as motivated as you.
- Always stay hungry. Never become complacent.
- Define success by being better at something than anyone else.
- Staying hungry when times are good will reward you when faced with challenges.
- Treat every issue as a challenge instead of an obstacle.

SECTION 5
LIVE YOUR LEADERSHIP

I like to say: every leader looks good when times are good. It's when things are bad that you really see great leadership.

From how I see things, leadership isn't something you impose on other people. The fact of the matter is, people want to be led—and more specifically, they want to be led by great leaders.

That's even more true when times are bad. When times are tough, that's when great leaders step up and keep everyone motivated and focused. They don't promote fear and anxiety. Instead, they help their team prepare for the better times ahead—which always come.

Another saying is that great leaders are born, not made. That suggests that you're a great leader because that's who you are and always have been. It's something that comes to you naturally.

I agree with that, but only to a certain extent. Yes, there

are some natural-born leaders—people who just happen to have leadership skills and abilities. But I also believe that great leadership skills can be taught, that anyone willing to listen to solid advice and guidance can, at the very least, become a better leader than they are right now.

Great leadership always goes hand in hand with great businesses. Here are some of the strategies I've learned and used over the years to improve my leadership skills—skills that you can improve, day in and day out, to help push your business toward the next level.

CHAPTER 13
IF YOU WANT TO LEAD, LISTEN FIRST

We were all born with two ears and one mouth for a good reason. And it isn't because nature just happened to have a second ear lying around that it decided to stick onto our heads.

No, the reason we have two ears and one mouth is that it's far more important to listen than it is to talk. That's true for everyone, but it's especially true for great leaders.

Great leaders take the time to listen—to partners, employees, advisors, and customers. In my case, I'll go talk to the people at the blackjack table or someone playing slots. A chat in the trenches can tell you a lot. You'll probably hear a fair amount of bullshit, but even if you get just one piece of useful information, you'll be a better leader. And the more you do it, the better you become at separating the useful from the useless.

Solid leaders know everyone has something of value to

contribute, so they make sure they give everyone the time and attention needed to truly be heard. That's because they know they'll become a better leader by listening.

This comes back to a central idea I've been emphasizing throughout this book: know what you know, and know what you don't. It's a form of personal honesty that every great leader embraces. They know what they know, and what they don't know, they're ready to learn or rely on others for that knowledge.

It's been said that great leaders surround themselves with people much smarter than they are. Do you then tune out and ignore these people? Of course not. When you assemble your team, ensure that every person has something of value to contribute. I use this exact strategy.

At the same time, this isn't to say that you shouldn't listen to your instincts. Far from it. Use your instincts and rely on them, particularly when you're listening to others. Your instincts will let you know what's good advice and what's not.

Or, for that matter, what is accurate and what is inaccurate.

But back to advisors for a moment. Now's a good time for me to share one of my pet peeves about business. To put it mildly, I'm not the biggest fan of hiring consultants. For one thing, they can be expensive. Many base their work on trying to make themselves increasingly indispensable—the more you work with them, the more you need them, and the more they get paid. No thanks!

"Consultants can consult you straight out of business."

Additionally, bringing an outsider into your business can often be counterproductive. Granted, they may offer you an objective perspective, but that's what you have other advisors for in the first place. Moreover, no one can possibly know more about your business than you and those who work with you every day. I see so many CEOs using consultants as a crutch.

Being a good listener also has many other advantages. Not too long ago, I had a meeting with managers and others who were in charge of several of my larger hotels. They were discussing a promotion in which hotel guests would receive 15 percent off the price of their stay. And they wanted to market it with the phrase "15 percent off BAR."

If you don't happen to be in the hotel business, when you hear that you would probably assume that phrase meant 15 percent off your tab at the hotel's bar. But that's not what we were trying to say. In this context, BAR refers to the price of the accommodations (the stated price of the room, or "best available rate").

Good thing I had been listening as closely as I had been. I reminded them to keep things simple.

"Guys, you all are putting hotel lingo in here," I said. "Somebody's going to walk into the bar and say, 'Where's my 15 percent off?' You may know that means your rate at your hotel, but they don't."

Listening to people around you means that you don't have to necessarily agree with or act on what other people tell you. Far from it. But at the very least, by taking into consideration what others have to say, you're giving yourself the best chance to make the smartest decisions possible. You've gained insight into some areas of your business that may need improvement. You've broadened your perspective, and that is never a bad thing to do.

Being a good listener helps a leader avoid insider business speak when communicating with the public. Sometimes a business is so inwardly focused that it overlooks times when it's using language that only its employees understand. Listening well cuts off that mistake before it can become a real problem.

I don't have many rules about the give-and-take with the people I meet with every single day. But I do have one I stick to religiously: never, ever hand me any bullshit. I can take good news, I can take bad news, but never try to dance around me with words whose only purpose is to hide or sweeten the truth. If you have something to say, just say it. I'm blunt with the people I work with, and I expect that kind of bluntness from them in return. Don't ever walk into my office and talk bullshit, because I will most definitely call you on it. That's because bullshit is, more often than not, easy to smell a mile away.

Here's an example. Some time back we had a restaurant in Oklahoma that, for whatever reason, wasn't performing well. I asked regional management what was going on. Well, said one, it's because there are "professional diners" in Oklahoma City.

I looked at him and said, "Excuse my bluntness, but what the f***?"

It was one of the craziest, most obvious bullshit comments I've ever heard in my life. Oklahoma City has "professional diners"— what does that even mean? What's a professional diner? Why is it exclusive to Oklahoma City? Cities like Houston, Austin, and Tulsa don't have professional diners.

To this day, I still don't understand what the hell he was trying to say. But in many ways, it doesn't matter. It was a bullshit answer, totally lacking in truth. I'd never heard such crap in my life. People are people everywhere. They expect good food and good service at a reasonable price. Obviously, we weren't doing that.

"Don't show a head in the bed if it's not there."

One of our sayings with regard to our hotels is "Don't show a head in the bed if it's not there." That is, don't play games with how many rooms you've sold on any given night. That's blunt and to the point, and that's the kind of bluntness I want from myself and everyone with whom I work. Being a good listener means you know what makes for good communication. Being blunt makes for efficient, clear-cut communication.

Being a good listener also cuts both ways. The best leaders listen closely to feedback they receive about their leadership skills. From there, they take it to heart to become better leaders. This comes back to the issue of being blunt—if you're blunt with the people you work with, don't just allow them to be blunt in return. Embrace it.

I've seen businesses on *Billion Dollar Buyer* where great products were essentially undercut by leaders who wouldn't listen to what their people had to say about their leadership style. I remember one business in particular where the business owner refused to believe that her leadership skills and interactions with others were the problem, even though comments from others labeled her "bossy," "silly," and "sophomoric."

In the end, I decided not to do business with that entrepreneur. And her leadership style was one of the primary reasons.

Committing to listening also doesn't mean you have to spend all day listening to others, particularly when they're going on too long or wandering endlessly off topic. If someone's not communicating clearly, ask them to make themselves clear. If they're blunt, it shouldn't take that long.

Speaking of efficiency, that's why I make it a policy to always have meetings that are as short as possible—ideally, fifteen minutes or less. Of course, we go over that time limit often, but trying to impose some sort of time restriction generally cuts back on the average time spent in meetings and keeps the time in the meeting productive. That, and we work to keep those short meetings consistent in how we review our business. That helps everyone prepare better to make the most of those few minutes.

The reason I believe so strongly in short meetings goes beyond the fact that everybody hates long, drawn-out sessions. A short meeting also promotes bluntness and accountability. If you're only asking people to focus for fifteen minutes or so, they bring their A game to those fifteen minutes. A lot gets done because it's focused and on point. The goal is to make them all focus for fifteen minutes and know that you're listening to them. Get to the point and get out.

Keeping meetings short is also valuable to reinforce an organization-wide commitment to ongoing goals and priorities.

For instance, since I've emphasized the value of hospitality, no matter the business, short meetings are an ideal way to reiterate that message. Use short meetings to remind everyone and to emphasize everything from the specials for that day to production and delivery priorities. Keep it short and on point, and the message is easy to convey and understand.

"People who ask questions are often the smartest in the room because they have the humility to ask about what they don't know."

As I said, I value people being blunt with me and vice versa. But, by the same token, I have no problem at all with someone telling me, "I don't know." I'm fine with that—it's blunt and to the point. I'd much rather hear "I don't know" than someone concocting some bullshit story. And I'm even finer with it if the person who says he or she doesn't know adds, "But I'm going to find out."

This comes back to the value of humility. None of us have all the answers, and the leader who recognizes that is well on his or her way to becoming a truly great leader. They're comfortable with someone telling them they don't know something, because they know they don't know everything themselves.

A leader who listens is also a connected leader, one in touch with his or her business and the people with whom he or she works.

A great leader also needs and wants to stay involved with his or her business, no matter how big the business may get. And to stay involved, my advice is always the same: keep your hands dirty.

By that, I mean stay committed to doing whatever is necessary to help your business succeed. It's never too small or trivial. In my case, if I walk into one of my establishments and see a candy wrapper on the floor, I pick it up. If I walk into one of my hotels and see a chair out of place, I always put it where it belongs.

The message here is, don't change who you are. If you see a problem, get involved. And that applies whether your business has grown by leaps and bounds or you're just starting out and having to do a lot yourself. Stay true to yourself.

LISTEN!

As a leader, never make the assumption that just because you told someone to do something, it's going to get done. That's one of the biggest lessons I have learned and that I share all the time. When you start out in business, make sure to follow up so that things are being done the way you want them done. And keep following up.

I did that myself, starting with my first business, and it remains true to this day. In fact, not too long ago, I was getting off the elevator at my Post Oak Hotel, when I passed a room service cart on the way to a room. When you're handling a room service order, lots of things can go wrong and, even worse, you can't just run back to the kitchen to get ketchup or a lemon that was left off the plate. So I always take the opportunity to look for things that aren't right.

I stopped the room service person. I looked to make sure the check was okay, which it was. The whole presentation on top of the cart looked good too. Then I asked to see the food.

The room service person took off the cover. Underneath was a burger that had no garnishes—no lettuce, tomatoes, pickles, nothing. It was just a hamburger bun with a burger and nothing else. It didn't meet my standards.

I went nuts. It was the worst presentation I had ever seen in my life. If I were at another hotel, I'd be laughing at them, but this was my hotel—The Post Oak—a Five Diamond hotel and one of the finest in the world, where they do 99 percent of everything right. But not this time.

I immediately took a picture of the food and shared it with the general manager of the hotel and the executive chef. The hotel had been winning all these awards left and right, and then we go and do something this stupid . . .

Like I said: never assume anything, even at a Five Diamond hotel. That's what I did there, at a place where you assume everything's going to be perfect. And it's the same thing I did some thirty years ago.

The goal is to stay involved at as many levels as you possibly can, right down to details that someone else might see as meaningless. Some business owners might see a piece of trash on the floor and figure it's not the end of the world—or wait until someone else does the dirty work and picks it up.

That's certainly not me, and I don't think that's you either. You want to be involved and are constantly looking for opportunities to stay involved.

The example I used earlier is being able to see a burned-out light bulb from forty thousand feet away. Many people might never even see that or, if they did, decide it's not important. But to me—and to almost every entrepreneur or business owner committed to succeeding—nothing is trivial, ever.

Think about what people, leaders included, look like when they're hard at work. They have their heads down. That's good—they're concentrating and focused. But it also pays to lift up your head once in a while and look around to see what's going on. Keeping your head on a swivel keeps you from missing anything of value.

And when you lift up your head, take the time to listen as closely as possible.

TILMAN'S TARGETS

- Take the time to listen to everyone. A great leader listens all the time.
- Be blunt with the people around you and expect them to do the same.
- Keep meetings short. Short meetings help people focus.
- Stay involved in your business as much as possible.
- Don't assume anything.

CHAPTER 14
BE A GREAT TEACHER

One day, I was sitting in a restaurant at the Golden Nugget in Lake Charles, Louisiana. As I mentioned in the previous chapter, it's critical for business owners at every level to remain involved in their businesses. With that in mind, I decided to wander around a bit to see what was going on elsewhere in the hotel.

As I walked around, I noticed one particular customer who had walked up to the front desk, apparently ready to check in. Everything seemed fine, so I moved on.

About thirty minutes later I went back down to the lobby and spotted that same customer sitting there. She obviously hadn't checked in, as her bags were still by her side.

I walked over to the front desk and asked what was going on. I was told there was "something not right in the room" that was holding everything up. Now I was genuinely curious, so I took the elevator up to the room to see what was happening.

As I walked up to the room, staff members were busy getting it ready. By all appearances, checking in shouldn't have been an issue.

"What's going on?" I asked one of the people.

"We're waiting for an iron for the room," she replied.

"What?"

"We're waiting for an iron for the room. Somebody hasn't signed off on it yet, and we can't get the iron in here until someone does."

I shook my head. "Do you mean we're going to let someone sit in the lobby for forty minutes—for an iron?" I demanded. The staff member shrugged.

As I looked around, I also noticed that other elements of the room were far from being guest ready. Apparently, everything had been slowed down or put on hold while the all-important decision about the iron was being made.

I hurried back down to the front desk and asked what other rooms were currently available in that class. There was one all ready to go, I was told, but it was being held for another guest—one who wouldn't be arriving until that evening, hours from now.

"I don't give a damn about the person coming in later," I told them. "Let's solve this issue right now. Let's not piss off the person who's already here! Let's put her in the room that's available, and we'll worry about the other person later."

Obviously, there had been a breakdown in communication. Somebody should have called in a senior manager, who probably could have fixed the situation in a few seconds, but nobody was thinking on their feet.

The good news was that I knew they could all learn from the experience. And that's why it's so important that great leaders also be great teachers.

How that teaching takes place will change every day. One day it may be a lesson learned from dealing with a crisis that never should have happened in the first place, like the guest stranded in the lobby needlessly waiting for a room. Others occur as a result of even more routine, everyday problems—a wet spot in front of the main entrance that takes too long to be mopped up, for instance.

As you deal with issues on a daily basis, don't be shy about explaining to the people around you how you arrived at the decision geared to solving that particular problem. Let them know the details of your thinking, so they can learn from how you thought things through.

That doesn't mean explaining every little decision. If there's a wet spot at the entrance, there's no need to show others how you found a towel and wiped it up. But you can share the lesson of always keeping your eyes open and constantly watching for small problems (chances are good that your staff already knows how to use a towel).

LISTEN!

The best way to sum up your goals as a teacher is to teach your people to act how you would act in a particular situation. If you're confident in your own ability to make decisions—and, as a business owner, you'd better be—use yourself as the template for teaching. If it works for you, don't be shy about sharing it with others.

Show them the value of making quick decisions as well. This comes back to knowing your business inside and out, from the numbers behind your business to your overall understanding of how things work and why. If you have that battery of knowledge at hand, you're better positioned to make fast decisions. You know what you're talking about and apply it in a practical manner.

Of course, that's not to say that all the decisions you make are going to be right. As we all know, running a business has enough surprises and unknowns to keep even the most informed entrepreneur from batting a thousand. But a mistaken decision can always be corrected, and people learn from that as much as they do from a decision that was right from the start. Often, that lesson from the wrong decision is even more valuable.

A quick decision not only promotes a sense of confidence about the business—a sense that leadership is connected and in control—it also teaches people the value of being able to think on their feet. This is as valuable a lesson as any that you can share with those with whom you work. Encourage people to use the knowledge they have to make decisions on the fly. Urge them to be creative and approach problems from new perspectives. Tolerate mistakes, as long as someone comes away having learned something from the experience.

Being able to think and act on the fly is a critical lesson because, for most businesses, no two days are exactly the same. Each day brings new challenges, new problems, and new issues that need to be addressed. These challenges require people with the ability to think as they move.

As we like to say around here to people interviewing for positions, if you want a script for every day, we don't have it. Every day is so new that any script would be pointless. I bet your business is in the same boat. That's the ideal situation for people with the ability to think on their feet.

That's one of the things I really liked about Brittany Hankamer and Megan Oberly of Eat Drink Host.

I first met the two women to learn about their custom paper products company. And I was very impressed by the quality and creativity they brought to the operation. (Who wouldn't like to be snacking off a small paper tray embossed with the words "Lil' Plate, Lil' Calories"?)

Further, the company passed my tests with flying colors. Prior to a Houston Rockets game, we offered fans a selection of paper and food-servings goods from both our usual stock and samples from Eat Drink Host. The results: 87 percent of fans responding said they preferred Eat Drink Host's products—a terrific result.

However, like many small businesses, they lacked sufficient scale to make their products affordable for operations such as mine. Still, I liked the design and offered $15,000 for exclusive rights to use the designs at Bill's Bar & Burger restaurants.

They accepted on the spot—no hemming and hawing, no getting-back-to-me nonsense. It wasn't the exact sort of deal they had been hoping for, but a quick assessment of the opportunity I offered them made them confident that this fast decision was the right one.

Or, as they might put it: Think. Fast. Succeed.

It's also helpful to be a hands-on teacher, one who works one-on-one whenever possible to help others learn and improve. I love working closely with my marketing and advertising people to show them how I think an ad or campaign might be improved. They may not love it as much as I do, but I like to think that everyone learns from it—including me.

Sometimes the best lessons are taught in an environment where not everyone is comfortable or, for that matter, happy. To drive home a message, I'll do certain things that, with the goal of teaching in mind, aren't particularly nice at the moment.

When we were still relatively small, we had a meeting of general managers. One of them explained that he was actively recruiting new employees and said he wanted to create his own logo to help do that.

I wasn't very happy. I told him in no uncertain terms that we had a marketing department and we already had a logo and it was in place for very good reasons. I said there was no way I was about to permit a new logo to distract from the overall message of the company.

I realized at the time that I was singling him out in front of the others. But I also realized that my meaning was absolutely clear—I knew that no one else in the room would ever do or even suggest something like that again.

Afterward, I went up to the general manager and apologized for how I had treated him. I told him I hadn't meant to be so hard on him but that he had given me an opportunity to drive home a message.

That's something that happens a great deal, and I always

make a point to put my arm around the person and explain why I did what I did. I want their memories about the experience to be short. I want their memory of the lesson learned to be long.

Another time, I was in one of my restaurants in San Antonio. I went into the kitchen and noticed silverware was in the garbage. It turned out that the servers and bussers getting rid of the remaining food on plates were also dumping silverware into the trash can.

I was so mad that I turned over the garbage and dumped it on the floor in front of everyone. With everyone in the kitchen watching, I got a busser and the manager, and the three of us picked up the trash, making sure to separate out the silverware. And, to make the busser feel a bit better, I tipped him twenty dollars.

That story underscores several important points. First, protect your assets. Second, when the owner of the company bends down to pick up trash, people start to pick up on a culture. They learn that everyone can and should do that sort of thing. That's when the managers start doing it, along with the waitstaff and everyone else. It's okay to get your hands dirty.

Although I believe in recognizing people who do their jobs well, teaching and ongoing contact with the people you work with shouldn't mean a never-ending rah-rah session. Great work should be recognized and rewarded, but remember, doing your job well is something to be expected, not constantly applauded. That comes back to culture. Your culture should mandate top performance. If employees do their jobs well, that's great, but that's also to be expected, not recognized as something special or out of the ordinary.

Taking a one-on-one approach should be applied to everyone with whom you work, not just certain people. One of my most important rules is simple and has everything to do with teaching: don't think that you're too important or too high up in a company to teach anyone. As I've said before, a great leader is always a humble leader, and that applies to teaching as much as it does to everything else.

In my restaurant division I tell my upper-level managers this: don't ever think you're too important or too busy to teach a busser or to help train a cook. Don't slough it off on your front managers or kitchen managers. Instead, take a busser, bring him over to a table, and explain clearly what you want him to do. You want him to wipe it off exactly like this. You want him to look at the base and see if there's any food down there—after all, people's feet deserve the same level of cleanliness as their hands do! Make sure there is no ketchup, little piece of butter, or anything else left in the seat because a kid was sitting there before.

That kind of teaching is invaluable. If a manager takes a busser and trains him or her, showing that circumstances and situations are always going to be different—and how to react— you can get more out of five or ten minutes' training than if the busser took part in a week of group instruction.

It also shows that employee something that's every bit as valuable as any part of the training—he or she is important. He or she feels valued and starts to think, *If the general manager is taking the time to show me how to do my job well, then this job is important to the success of the entire business.*

"Don't ever think that your position is too high to teach others. Because I still teach every single day. And, just as important, I learn as much as I teach others."

Every day is an experience in learning for me as well as everyone else. Somebody always does something in a day that makes me a little bit smarter than I was when the day began. If you're a leader who's dedicated to teaching everyone around all that you have to share, you can be every bit as open to learning and benefitting from all they can offer in return.

What makes a good learner? Being able to stop and listen. I know that if I take the time to listen, and I can pick up even one little thing each and every day, I'm going to be a better entrepreneur, owner, manager, employee—whatever—the next day.

TILMAN'S TARGETS

- A great leader is also a great teacher. Take every opportunity to teach those around you.
- Encourage people to think on their feet and be creative.
- Don't be afraid to make mistakes. Mistakes can be a more effective teacher than success.
- Great leaders are always learning.

CHAPTER 15
CHANGE, CHANGE, CHANGE

M any people, including entrepreneurs, are frightened or intimidated by change.

Not me. I love change. In fact, I love to say, "Change, change, change."

Change gives every one of us the opportunity to improve, to reinvent ourselves, and to correct past mistakes. And, if you don't change, then change some more, the paddle I mentioned at the beginning of this book is going to find your ass.

And fast.

Think back to the prior chapter that discussed the importance of being a great teacher. The reason it's vital to be teaching all the time is that you want the people around you to change and grow. You want them to improve, to get better at their jobs, and to think faster and more creatively on their feet.

> ### LISTEN!
>
> The simple fact of the matter is that change occurs constantly, whether you like it or not. You can either learn to anticipate change and put you and your business in a better position to react with greater agility, or you can ignore and deny change.

And, like I mentioned at the beginning of this chapter, that can lead to one nasty paddling. Just ask companies like Xerox, Kodak, and Blockbuster—iconic names that chose to ignore the change that was all around them. The paddle certainly found them.

The presence and importance of change is something I preach constantly. It's critical that you're always looking for ways to change your business, because industries are constantly being disrupted, and trends are constantly changing everything around us. If you're not looking for ways to get ahead of the curve with new cutting-edge products or services, you can fall behind all too easily. So, instead of looking up and finding you're behind the curve, get out in front of it whenever you can.

Coca-Cola is a good example. Once a company that produced a soft drink, they've changed to incorporate all sorts of different drinks and products, not to mention the design and look of those products. Could they have survived if they had stuck to that one type of drink? Probably, but their capacity to change has allowed the company to excel.

Coca-Cola's example also points out the importance of

anticipating change. The company realized their market was changing in all sorts of ways, and they were ready with products to greet that change.

"By anticipating change, you don't just change with the times—you change the times themselves."

My businesses change constantly, be it their menu items, staff uniforms, music that's played, or layout and feel. When I acquired Morton's The Steakhouse in 2011, although they'd been a popular place for steaks since their first restaurant in 1978, by the time I bought the concept, they had seventy-plus steakhouses failing to do one critical thing: change, change, change.

One of the most world-renowned steakhouse brands out there still looked and felt like it did thirty years before. Red leather banquettes, dark mahogany wood everywhere, maître d's with bowties in tuxedoes, no music, and even a food cart they rolled out to every table to show off their raw steaks at the beginning of service. The brand needed to attract a broader customer base.

By 2011, the likes of Del Frisco's, Mastro's, STK, and other high-end steakhouses had passed Morton's by on look, feel, and vibe. So what did I do? Change, change, change. I gave them an entirely new interior design, installed modern furniture, updated the uniforms (killing the bowties and tuxedoes), turned down the lights, turned on the music, and expanded the menu. And what happened? I grew the customer base and did more business. The same people who knew and loved the brand kept coming, and I introduced Morton's to an entirely new generation of customers who used to think that Morton's was where their grandparents ate on their wedding anniversary.

How can you anticipate change? To quote the title of my book—"Shut up and listen!"

LISTEN!

Pay attention to changes in society, such as greater interest in healthy, farm-to-table foods. Understand your customer base. What do they value right now? Pay attention to technology trends and innovations. Which ones do you expect will boost the value and appeal of your business? Talk to your customers. Talk to your employees—the greater the variety of people you speak with, the broader and more accurate the picture of change you can anticipate and react to.

Failing to beat change to the punch puts change in the position of dictating terms to you, rather than the other way around. And like I always say, if you sit on your hands, you're going to go out of business.

Here's an example that shows the importance of being open to change. The Supreme Court recently allowed states to implement various sorts of legalized sports gambling. As you probably know, a good portion of my overall business operation has to do with gambling, such as gaming tables, slot machines, and the like.

On one hand, we could choose to hunker down and stick with what we already have in place, hoping that legalized sports gambling doesn't detract from the gambling we already have. On the other hand, we could embrace this type of change as a fresh avenue of opportunity, and that's exactly what we have done.

During a CNBC interview about the topic, I summed it up this way: "We all have to evolve."

That's an ideal summary of my approach to change. It's going to happen, so put yourself and your business in a position to make the most of it.

Every business deals with change on an ongoing basis. In the restaurant business, it's everything from making the music a little bit louder to incorporating communal tables to adding dishes like avocado toast and shishito peppers that reflect how people want to eat today.

That raises an obvious question: When is change good, and when is it better to keep doing what you've been doing? The answer is easy: test. If you've watched *Billion Dollar Buyer*, almost every episode has at least one instance where we put a small company's product up against competitors. Then, using everyone from real customers to others who work for me, we ask them to be honest. What's better and why?

That emphasis on going to your customers to evaluate change is critical. For one thing, you're going to get honest feedback. Just as important, you're listening to the people who may or may not buy your product—not listening to yourself or the people with whom you work. And, as I said in an earlier chapter, that's one of the best ways to cater to the masses. Offer them what they want.

Two final bits of advice. When I test products against other products, I require an 80 percent result to justify any sort of change. For instance, if we're testing a new salad dressing with ten participants, a minimum of eight out of ten of those folks need to say they prefer the new dressing for us to even consider a switch. That high level of approval gives greater certainty to any decision that's made. It helps identify change that truly makes sense.

The second bit of advice is, if change involves eliminating something, never cut anything that's going to affect your customer.

Earlier I discussed how you can grow your business by cutting expenses. That's a proven strategy, but don't worsen the customer experience in the process.

For instance, if you operate a restaurant, automatically putting bread on a table can cost a surprising amount of money. Instead, ask if they want bread. That's not lessening the customer experience—rather, it's refining it by letting the customer decide. There's cost cutting involved, but not at the expense of the customer experience.

By the same token, a company that switches to smaller, more cost-efficient delivery vehicles isn't impacting customers. They're still going to receive the same product, just in a different manner. If the product arrives on schedule and is followed up with helpful customer support, nothing about what the customer sees changes.

How else do you best react to and leverage change? One

proven strategy is to put people in the right positions in your company, where they can make the most of their skills and other attributes to use change to your advantage.

This relates to a critical issue I discussed earlier in the book. Any successful business requires a balance of experience and skills—you need a numbers guy, you need a creative guy, that sort of balance. That balance is essential when a problem or issue crops up where a certain kind of knowledge is necessary for a solution—the kind of problem or issue that reflects some sort of change. With the right kind of balance, there is already someone in place to make a good decision.

Balance is vital when confronting change. Change brings opportunity, but it can also bring uncertainty, instability, and even chaos. Having the right people in positions that make the best use of their skills can be the difference between taking your business to the next level as a result of the change or struggling because change overwhelmed you.

Think back to the story I shared about banks closing left and right throughout Texas in the 1980s. As someone with significant financial commitments with many of those institutions, it would have been possible for my business to go under as quickly as many of those banks.

But it didn't happen. That's because I reacted to that sweeping change with the goal of using it to my advantage rather than suffering and struggling like so many others. The change was occurring, whether I liked it or not. As it turned out, I was able to like it! Further, change that brought disaster to so many others proved a valuable education for me. I learned not only the essential value of always having cash on hand but also the need to look past the chaos of change to identify opportunities others were too freaked out to notice.

The ability to lead and the obstacles that change brings go hand in hand. I like to say that you could have the greatest product or the greatest anything, but it all comes down to the people who are working with that product. No product or service is so unique or so amazing that it can be successful in and of itself. It takes people to make that happen.

You have great companies today that have failed because of the people who were running them. You also have companies that are extremely successful because of the people who are running them. And if you switched the people around, the business that used to be successful might be out of business. Meanwhile, the ones who struggled may be doing great. It all comes down to putting the right people in place, one of the greatest challenges that any leader faces.

There are many ways to evaluate people to help you select the right people for the right jobs. I've found that no matter the specifics of the situation, there's a rule of thumb you can't go wrong with: hire people who are stronger than you, and don't be intimidated by them.

This touches on a business issue that leaders have been wrestling with forever. Every business leader wants to hire the most talented people available. Even though that may look like an obvious thing to do, it can also mean hiring someone who, over time, is so damn talented that they end up taking your job from you. That can be threatening.

"One of the things about being a good leader is hiring people who are stronger than you, and if you hire people who are stronger than you, they'll never take your job. They'll help you keep your job."

My advice: relax and choose the best people you possibly can. They'll help you keep your job by performing to the best of their abilities in their own jobs. They may require less hands-on guidance, freeing you up to pay attention to other things. Thinking on their feet and making quick decisions may come naturally to them.

Great leaders are comfortable with the very best people around them because they know that the most talented people are those best equipped to anticipate and make the most of the change that's constantly occurring.

But don't make hiring smarter people a crutch, a situation where you can leave them to do all the heavy lifting, so you can look good. It's critical to maintain your work ethic—otherwise that smarter person might, in fact, take your job. And, if that happens, you have no one to blame but yourself.

Be sure to rely on your experience when taking steps to hire the most talented people possible. That's because someone, however smart or skilled, may not have the same level of experience as you. Not only can that valuable experience help keep you secure in your job, the combination of your hands-on savvy with another's great potential can make for a powerful team.

It's also essential to differentiate between meaningful change and fads. Fads tend to stick out as the short-term craze that they are—they have little in the way of genuine usefulness. For instance, *Angry Birds* may have been all the rage for a while, but that fad migrated as quickly as it came. Gluten-free food, on the other hand, has scientific reason behind it. People feel better eating that way. That's no fad.

Another misstep I see among business leaders, particularly younger entrepreneurs, is a tendency to overreact. I've been around long enough to know that the best decision is sometimes no decision at all. Always work toward having all the information you need to make the right decision, but if you don't have that kind of information, no decision is the best kind of decision—or, by the same token, the issue at hand is simply going to go away on its own.

Let me give you an example. Recently, Texas passed a law that anybody can carry a gun. Without getting into the politics of it, many businesses were struggling with how they should react to the new law. If they didn't agree with the new regulations, should they put up signs in all of their businesses saying that customers can't bring guns into their establishments? How could they communicate with customers if they agreed with the new law? What if they were somewhere in the middle, neither entirely in support or opposition?

In this instance, it was far better for us to do nothing. We reasoned it was much smarter to see how hot this topic remained and to let it play itself out. Why alienate any of our customers—no matter their politics—when the issue would likely cool down and resolve itself?

Which is exactly what it did.

Things have a way of working out on their own, and it's valuable for business owners and entrepreneurs to recognize that and give the situation ample time to develop.

It boils down to a simple rule about leadership and change: don't overthink things. That's not to say you shouldn't know your numbers inside and out, or that you shouldn't do the most complete due diligence you can. But don't go overboard. Don't make an issue needlessly complicated by overthinking it.

Call it the 95:5 rule, call it the good old KISS principle (Keep It Simple, Stupid), but don't needlessly waste your energy on issues that don't warrant it. And that can include change—the one certainty about business that we can accept with the same level of certainty.

TILMAN'S TARGETS

- Change, change, change.
- A great leader accepts change.
- Don't be afraid to hire people who are smarter or more talented than you.
- Sometimes the best decision is no decision at all.
- Don't overthink. Allow things to play out.

CONCLUSION

Don't Choose to Quit—Choose to Keep Punching

When you strip away everything else related to running a successful business—great product, great customer service, terrific marketing—one additional factor can separate a business with growth potential from one that dies.

Persistence—the ability to keep going, no matter how challenging the circumstances or what others might be saying.

Reading this, you might be tempted to say that it's easy for me to talk about the value of hanging in there. But remember, it wasn't always like this for me—far from it. Back when I was getting started, I scrambled constantly. Finding the money to fuel my business growth was an enormous challenge unto itself.

I also believe that there are few successful business owners who don't have similar stories to share—entrepreneurs who kept plugging away when others might have long before thrown in the towel.

That's why I want to wrap up this book with a breakout strategy that may be simple to understand but challenging to live by: never, ever give up. That's the reason this topic is at the end of the book. The ability to keep going and never give up is that important. Long after you finish reading, I want you to remember this strategy, even if you don't recall everything else I've told you.

And who knows? One day you may be able to look back and tell some young entrepreneur about the struggles you went through before you hit it big!

A number of episodes of *Billion Dollar Buyer* feature small businesses with a common issue: they're struggling to succeed.

The reasons for those struggles can vary. Some businesses are victims of themselves—young entrepreneurs who want too much, too fast. Others suffer because they don't understand the numbers that relate to their business—a flaw I repeatedly point out.

Then there are those businesses that have hit some tough breaks, such as the Houston-based granite company that was teetering on the edge of failure because of Hurricane Harvey, which I discuss later.

Although the circumstances differ, I inevitably come back to a central message.

LISTEN!

Keep going. No matter what. You never know—the other guy might go down before you do.

My own story about the Texas banking situation in the 1980s is a great example of why it pays to keep punching. In my case, as you'll remember, I was able to fly under the radar and keep growing my businesses, while regulators dealt with the bigger issue of a rash of lenders who were shutting their doors.

In the end, I survived. Most of them didn't.

That's a valuable lesson. Keep punching because the other guy might get knocked out first. In my case, the "other guy" was a bunch of banks. In your case, it might be a competitor, or a creditor, or an internal production issue. So long as you stay alive, you've got a chance to outlast that other guy or solve a lingering problem.

Throughout this book, I've talked about a variety of skills that you need to be a successful entrepreneur and, ultimately, grow your business. I consider persistence—the willingness to keep punching—as important a skill as any other you may have.

Some people are naturally more persistent than others. But I truly believe that persistence is a skill and an attribute that business leaders can learn.

Ignore the naysayers! No matter who or where you are, you're going to encounter people who are all too quick to point out all that you're fighting against and encourage you to throw in the towel. Some may be motivated out of genuine concern, while others may have different reasons for urging you to quit.

You want to hang in there and keep punching and keep reminding yourself what you're good at. Work to build that strength even further. And it may even help you pinpoint why your business is misfiring. I remember when my business was struggling, and I told my managers we need to get back to the basics: hot food hot and cold food cold. That became our theme. From that point on, our customers knew what they were going to get, and we were going to do it well.

Another strategy to keep you in the fight is to never let any current struggles cloud past success. For example, maybe your product or service received a great response when you first started your business. It stands to reason that customers saw something in that product that they valued—that should boost your confidence and commitment. There's something there worth fighting for.

Focusing on early success can also be a helpful guidepost to pinpoint why you may be floundering now. Ask yourself: "What's changed from the time when things were going really, really well?" Are you doing something differently that's turned success into struggle?

Staying in the fight also requires that you be the bull—another strategy I covered. This means you're the source of strength for the business, a leader whose best features and attributes come out when everything around you seems to be going straight to hell. This is when leaders pull themselves up by their bootstraps. Leaders stand tall in tough times. Be the bull who helps keep others upbeat and makes them feel genuinely vested in the business's survival and growth.

And one other thing about bulls—they rarely throw in the towel and, if they do, it's never too early.

When I see businesses of all sorts close up shop, it's often not so much a matter of being outpunched by someone else. Instead, it's submitting, throwing up your hands and declaring it's all over way too early.

As I said, you can be outpunched in business. Maybe you've run completely out of cash, or your lenders will no longer extend you credit.

In my experience, rather than choosing to keep fighting through whatever obstacles they may be facing, some businesses choose instead to close up shop.

The reality is that many of them don't have to do that, as I witnessed firsthand not too long ago. And I'm glad I was able to convince this business to stay in the game.

The final episode of season three of *Billion Dollar Buyer* featured K & N Custom Granite, a Houston-based supplier of granite and remodeling materials for both home and commercial use.

And they nearly went under—both literally and figuratively.

A genuine mom-and-pop operation—a husband and wife team, Gus and Jessica Trevino—K & N was devastated by Hurricane Harvey, which slammed the Houston area and other parts of the Gulf Coast in 2017. The damage lingered for weeks—with roads impassably flooded, the Trevinos were stranded in their home for fourteen days, unable to get to their shop. When they did finally manage to get to their business, they counted themselves fortunate that no water had gotten into the facility.

But the damage was done in other ways. Having struggled even before the storm struck, jobs that had been lined up prior to the storm's arrival couldn't be completed. They lost their largest account. Consequently, the business was forced to shut down for almost three weeks, costing them anywhere from $75,000 to

$100,000—no small amount when sales for the prior year totaled less than $700,000.

Even worse, since they were such a small operation, catching up was almost impossible. No plan B was in place, just a desperate scramble to keep going from one day to the next.

Things were so bad that when I first met Jessica and Gus, they told me they were seriously thinking about filing Chapter 11 and closing up shop.

My reaction was: What are you talking about?

Their door was still open, I told them. I see a bunch of stone outside. There's nothing preventing customers from walking in and placing orders.

I said you're not out of business until you don't have the last dollar to go out and buy product—until somebody comes and padlocks this door, or you can't make payroll. That's it. And if you can't make payroll, you have to do it all—be the salesman, the manufacturer, everything. But you are in business!

I also told them not to waste their money on an attorney. I was confident that Jessica and Gus could pick themselves up off the turf and do what amounted to an in-house restructuring.

I also threw down a challenge to let them see for themselves what they could do, even under enormous financial pressures. I asked them to design a bar countertop with a bullnose cut. They delivered.

The bar showed off terrific craftsmanship and color. It was just what I was looking for and, in return, I proposed that they become the priority stone vendor for one of my casinos and for three restaurants—a deal worth $200,000.

They accepted.

Gus and Jessica's story illustrates a key strategy behind a determination to keep going when giving up might seem the obvious answer. In their case, they didn't go out of business, and I am happy that I had a role in that decision.

When faced with adversity, is a business closing its doors because conditions dictate it, or are the owners shutting down because they no longer have the fight?

"You're not out of business until you don't have the last dollar to go out and buy product to make, until somebody comes and padlocks your door, or you can't make payroll."

This is similar to an earlier discussion we had about customer service. When you or someone else in your business tells a customer no, is saying no a choice or something that's completely beyond control? As we've covered, it's often the case of someone choosing to say no rather than having to.

It's the same in dealing with challenges that seem to threaten the life of your business. Are you deciding to close because you have to or because you choose to?

Giving up is easy, particularly when compared to the effort and sacrifice that it can take to keep a business alive. Many business owners reason—or convince themselves—that they've done all they can. Why fight against something that seems unbeatable?

But as I often remind entrepreneurs, you'd be surprised to see how long it takes to actually go out of business. By that, I don't mean choosing to lock the doors one day and letting it go at that. Instead, what I mean is that it can take an awfully long time before it becomes impossible to keep a business open. You may struggle to pay your rent, you may have to forgo paying yourself, and you may have to take on jobs and responsibilities that you never in a million years saw yourself doing.

It comes back to making good decisions and thinking outside the box.

Here's an out-of-the-box strategy I successfully used, called an "in the drawer judgment."

Let's say you owe a manufacturer $30,000. You need to obtain more product from that manufacturer but don't have the $30,000 you owe him. If you're thinking outside the box, you might approach the manufacturer and say, "I can't pay you the $30,000 I owe you right now, but I'm going to agree to an in the drawer judgment, so if I ever miss a payment again, you can collect on the judgment.

"But you've got to sell me product. If you don't, I'm out of business. If you do, I'm going to pay you $2,500 a month for the next twelve months, and you're going to get your money. But if you don't do this for me, you're never going to get paid."

That's thinking outside the box. One of the keys to making good decisions is bearing in mind how the other person stands to benefit. It's a simple scenario—either you both win, or you both lose.

Say the manufacturer agrees to your proposal. Next, you've got to deal with a landlord to whom you owe three months' back rent. Again, work the deal so you both stand to benefit. Ask if she can give you a 50 percent rent cut for the next three months. Tell her she can apply it on the back end to what you owe her, if she gives you a year to catch up. And—here's the kicker—if you don't perform for even one month, tell her you're happy to sign an agreement giving her the right to kick you out. No need to padlock the door or get a sheriff's deputy—you're out, and that's that.

Is all that risky? Of course. Creative thinking and making solid decisions are two of your biggest weapons if you're persistent.

The conclusion: remind yourself that the way to the top is almost never by way of a straight, unbroken line.

Did you really, truly expect to rocket right out of the gate with no bumps and bruises along the way? Granted, things now may seem darker than you ever anticipated, but bear in mind that everyone has to struggle occasionally.

Looking to others for support and advice can also be critical at this juncture. That's what I did with the Trevinos. Talk with other entrepreneurs. Get feedback from people who can provide an objective viewpoint, which can also be helpful in making the right decision for your business.

However helpful outside advice can be, bulls recognize that they are their own best-trusted advisors.

Don't quit, unless there's absolutely no other choice. Keep punching.

I promise you'll be surprised. You've got a lot more breaths in you than you might think.

And always remember, the best asset you have is your own instinct.

TILMAN'S TARGETS

- Leaders stand tall in tough times.
- Persistence is a valuable skill—keep punching.
- Always think outside the box.
- When things are hard, remember the basics.
- Always be the bull.

AFTERWORD

"Now That You've Listened..."

N ow that we're at the end of this book, I have a confession to make.

When we were trying to decide on a title, first we did all the usual research and legwork to try to identify a phrase that captured several important things.

Second, we wanted to have a title that sounded like me. I think we got that covered!

But a third component was something I feel strongly about. And that, for better or worse, is frustration.

I cannot tell you how frustrating it is for me to try to share all that I've learned with entrepreneurs and others who are looking to take their businesses to the next level—to try to share what I can with them, only to have them refuse in one way or another to take my advice to heart.

That's frustrating as hell to me. I didn't make the Forbes list because my name is Rockefeller. I am self-made and started out just like you. And, like the title of this book says, it makes me want to scream, "Shut up and listen!"

That's not vanity. That's not being self-indulgent. My ideas and strategies have worked for me and can work for you.

I've shared successful ideas and strategies that I've experienced in over thirty-five years in business. My job with this book is to help you grow your business and spare you from making costly mistakes.

And avoiding costly mistakes can boil down to remembering what my friends refer to as "Tilmanisms"—phrases and ideas that I say over and over:

"You might think you know what you're doing, but I'm going to show you what you don't know."

"Be plappy."

"Build a few hours or days into your schedule for the what-ifs. If I tell somebody I'm going to deliver something on this day, I'm damn well going to deliver it. I'm going to make that customer feel special."

"Why is it so easy to say no when you can say yes?"

"There are no spare customers."

"The biggest issue that small businesses face involves working capital, because they have to pay for everything up front."

"When things are bad, eat the weak and grow your business."

"Never put your lifestyle ahead of the growth of your business."

"Know your numbers. Numbers don't lie."

"I can look at a business and its numbers and within a few minutes know if that business has the stuff to become really successful. It's what I'm good at, and I know this."

"Never become partners with someone who has the same skill set as you."

"You're trying to run a marathon, and you haven't even shown me you can crawl."

"No matter the circumstances, be the bull."

"Consultants can consult you straight out of business."

"Don't show a head in the bed if it's not there."

"People who ask questions are often the smartest in the room because they have the humility to ask about what they don't know."

"Don't ever think that your position is too high to teach others. Because I still teach every single day. And, just as important, I learn as much as I teach others."

"By anticipating change, you don't just change with the times—you change the times themselves."

"One of the things about being a good leader is hiring people who are stronger than you, and if you hire people who are stronger than you, they'll never take your job. They'll help you keep your job."

"You're not out of business until you don't have the last dollar to go out and buy product to make, until somebody comes and padlocks your door, or you can't make payroll."

And, of course, "Shut up and listen!"

Now that you've reached the end of all my preaching, it's obvious that you also saw the value of shutting up and listening—a maxim we can all stand to use in both our businesses and our lives in general.

So, since you did shut up and listen, I now can shut up too.

And say thank you for letting me share what I know will be of value to you and your business—today, tomorrow, and in the years ahead.

THE TILMAN I KNOW

Mike Milken

Michael Milken is a name you probably know well. He revolutionized the bond business in the 1980s and is currently building the Center for the American Dream in Washington, DC. Mike is a dear friend of mine, who embraces the value of selling to the masses.

"Tilman understands what the business is but also understands the consumer. A lot of people offer products that the consumer might not want, but they think consumers want. Tilman has the ability to see the world through other people's eyes. A lot of people only see the world through their own eyes, and as a result, they don't always get an accurate picture of the world.

"When Tilman acquired the Golden Nugget in Las Vegas, he knew he had to define a broader customer, a broader market. What was in place was too targeted. He did the same thing in Atlantic City and Biloxi, Mississippi—defining the market for what it is, not what it was. And since Tilman bought those, they've never looked back. It's a matter of understanding what the customer wants.

"You also see it on his *Billion Dollar Buyer* show. He's very blunt. He just tells the people the truth, that certain ideas just won't work. Viewers might think he's just bursting other people's bubbles, but one of the most important things you can ever do is to let a person know up front that what they're trying to do is going to be very, very, very difficult. Don't risk losing your family savings on an idea that just won't work.

"What Tilman provides on the show is honesty, insightfulness, and a world of wisdom—not just for the person who wants to be in that business and sell to him but for the person who's thinking about going into business. He's very symbolic of the American Dream."

Scott Kelly

Scott Kelly is a retired astronaut and author of the bestselling book *Endurance: My Year in Space, a Lifetime of Discovery*, which details a year he spent in outer space. (Talk about knowing about the 5 percent that makes things amazing!) He was with me one time when I identified the 5 percent in a particular business:

"Tilman and I were having a drink. The bartender—a very professional bartender who obviously took his work very seriously—hand poured the vodka into our glasses without bothering to measure with a shot glass. He gave us our drinks, and we both took a sip.

"'How much vodka is in that?' Tilman asked suspiciously. The bartender replied that it was exactly two ounces. At Tilman's request, he poured some vodka into a glass without measuring it.

"'Get a shot glass,' Tilman suggested. The bartender did so and poured the vodka into the shot glass. It was just a bit short of a full shot—the two ounces the bartender was so confident he had been serving.

"How Tilman knew that the bartender wasn't pouring a full shot, I have no idea, but that's one of the reasons for his success. Literally no detail is too small for him."

Rich Handler

My friend Rich Handler, CEO of the Wall Street–based Jefferies Group, knows the value of friendship. Rich and I first met during a time when capital was exceedingly difficult to come by. It helped cement a friendship that has lasted to this day.

"We met in the depth of a financial crisis—there was basically no functional capital environment. We figured a way to backstop a deal. But, we also developed a very personal bond. With Tilman, business and life are very much intertwined. Since we were able to help him, he's repaid us with extreme loyalty."

Rich adds that people who see business as wholly separate from personal relationships can miss out on an exceedingly powerful business tool:

"People who are transactional in nature can't see that. If you're Tilman's friend—in business or in life—you'll find that he's an incredibly loyal person. That works out for him, and it works out for the friend."

Dave Jacquin

Dave Jacquin is the founder of North Point Advisors. North Point is one of the leading consumer mergers and acquisitions firms in the United States. I've worked with them extensively over the years. When it comes to hunger, Dave is often at a loss to explain why I keep going the way I go.

"To me, Tilman is like Michael Jordan. If I were him and I had his money, I can't tell you how done I would be. But he's never done. He always bets on himself and delivers. He creates value across the board. And he makes it pay off."

But Dave also recognizes the example a hungry leader sets for those around him. He sees a simple but powerful formula: be hungry and make sure those around you are hungry as well.

"Tilman is the hardest-working guy I know. He really leads by example. You can't be on his team if you can't keep up."

But some things are far more important than a rigorous work regimen, Dave adds:

"I had open heart surgery about a year ago. I wake up, and there's Tilman sitting at the end of my bed."

Al Lewis

A bull is also eager to find common ground with everyone, understanding that positive relationships with others are a critical component of success, now and in the future. In fact, some of the most valuable friendships are built with people who at one time were anything but friendly.

Some fifteen years back, I acquired the financially strapped Denver Aquarium. At that same time, I had some disagreements with the city regarding taxes on the property, and one day, while doing an earnings conference call when Landry's was a public company, I threatened to bulldoze the building if the city didn't lower the property taxes. I said it for drama, just to make a point.

That's when Al Lewis entered my world—with both elbows flying.

A business columnist for the *Denver Post*, he let me have it with both barrels. He labeled me a "big carp" and a mercenary "seafood cowboy." He urged me, in words probably watered down by the time they reached the pages of the newspaper, to go home to Texas and stay there.

A year later, The Aquarium reopened, the beneficiary of a $20 million infusion to improve the facility and add other attractive features, such as a full-service restaurant.

And, never one to hold a grudge, I invited the saber-keyboarded Mr. Lewis to join us at the opening—which, to his credit, he attended.

Things can certainly change in a year. Calling me the man who he believed "saved" The Aquarium, he wrote a follow-up column. Having spent some time with me at the opening, Lewis wrote, "We got along so well that I wanted to give him a pucker little fish kiss."

What happened? I recognized that he had a job to do and, for his part, he knew I had to do mine.

"You're not mad I called you a carp?" he asked at one point in the evening.

"You get paid to write interesting things," I replied, confessing that I knew full well the kind of "drama" my spat with the taxing authorities would kick up. "I knew I would get drama out of it when I said it, and you knew you would get drama out of it when you wrote it. You and I are a lot alike."

Some years later, Al and I met again; this time he was working as the business editor for the *Houston Chronicle*. That was followed by another column in which he wrote the following: "If someone is poking fun at you or challenging you, they obviously care. Who knows, they may turn out to be helpful in the end."

And by this time Al had changed from calling me "carp" and "shark" to "angelfish."

You may not have much in common with many of the people with whom you have to deal, but it's always a good idea to find as much common ground as possible. Try to walk around in their shoes a bit. That's because friends can be one of the most valuable advantages to building a successful business. An enemy rarely is.

Abraham Lincoln himself knew that. Once admonished for being too kind to his enemies, he supposedly said he would "destroy" them.

By making them his friends.

Mark Kelly

Several years back, you might recall that Arizona congresswoman Gabrielle (Gabby) Giffords was shot in an attempted assassination. Gabby is married to my good friend, astronaut Mark Kelly (Scott's brother). I immediately went to work making arrangements to get Mark and his family to Arizona.

While the plane was in the air, I was watching CNN. All of a sudden it was reported that Gabby had died. Mark had said that Gabby was stable and in surgery with a head injury. Since none of her other vital organs were impacted by the shooting, it made no sense to me that she could have died. Since I knew Mark would be watching the news story from the plane, I immediately contacted him and told him I was 100 percent sure she was still alive.

But, just as important, my gut told me that all those news reports were wrong. And Mark appreciated my ability to see that.

"Tilman said he knew Gabby was still alive, and he was right. You see that same sort of decisiveness and intuition in other parts of his life. He also has an uncanny ability to see the world through the eyes of others, understanding and anticipating what people want."

Renu Khator

Change has been the name of the game at the University of Houston under the leadership of Chancellor Renu Khator. During her tenure, UH has experienced record-breaking research funding, enrollment, and academic excellence. And I've been fortunate to be involved as chairman of the university's board of regents for the past five years. Chancellor Khator and I both are firm believers in the power of change for the better.

"With Tilman's last five years as chairman of the board of regents, we have seen a difference in the university that we have never seen before. Tilman is the ideal leader for a public institution. He asks very precise questions, and he always gives you direction. His vision is so big, so powerful, so bold. He offers up ideas that none of us ever thought of."

One example is the university's decision to break ground in 2018 for a satellite campus in Katy, Texas, despite the fact that the community had no existing higher education facilities.

"Tilman said, 'I know where people are going to be living ten and twenty years from now.' He knows how essential it is to bring the product to the people."

I felt it was essential to expand the scope of the university's programs to address locations that are going to experience significant population growth—again, the idea of serving the masses.

Likewise with the university's football program, long viewed as a stepping-stone for jobs at bigger, more visible programs. Working with Chancellor Khator, we've implemented a new buyout program designed to build mutual loyalty between the university and promising new hires.

"Tilman said, 'Let's change the business model, so there's a real commitment between the university and coaches.'

"He's increased the efficiency of everything that we do, including board of regents meetings. People come prepared for those meetings now, which is not always the case in a public institution.

"If I have to define one quality about Tilman, it's his compassion. Once we had a student who tried to commit suicide. Tilman texted me every four hours asking how the student was doing. His heart really connects with the students because he knows people are not just numbers.

"The way Tilman thinks from a business standpoint has put the University of Houston on a completely different trajectory."

ABOUT THE AUTHOR

Tilman Fertitta, a Houston native, is an accomplished businessman and recognized as a world leader in the dining, hospitality, entertainment, and gaming industries. *Forbes* referred to him as "the richest restauranteur in the world." Fertitta is the star of his own reality TV show on CNBC, *Billion Dollar Buyer*, and is also the sole owner of Fertitta Entertainment, which owns the restaurant giant Landry's, the Golden Nugget Casinos and Hotels, and the NBA's Houston Rockets.

erine held her briefly, aware that there were tears coursing down her own cheeks, blinding her, making her shake. Already, as they swayed together for a moment, her plans were changing. Food first, then get out. Anywhere, just out, even in the dark, dressed as they were, out. Away. It was suddenly obvious there would be no end to this, no finale apart from a fading away and in that brief embrace, of desperate love and affection, Katherine could feel the sharp edge of a rib cage, more poignant and revealing than any tears. The child was thin, horribly thin, and the cough a rasp of accusation.

Softly, she closed the door of the kitchen. The pair of them, Katherine in particular, suffering from the peculiar desire to laugh, the kind of giggles accompanying a midnight feast, although, despite her still persisting nausea, Katherine had found from nowhere a clear head and considerable authority. Jeanetta clutched her skirt, refusing to move from her side. "Now," she whispered to Jeanetta, "eat as slowly as you can: you don't want to be sick, we haven't time." Katherine had always been vague about food suitable for her children, gave them whatever she had, but in the 2:00 A.M. clarity, saw how cornflakes were the best she could offer in all their digestible blandness. With even more uncharacteristic forethought, she placed two apples in the handbag she had left earlier in the kitchen, thinking ahead with furious planning. There was a thin summer coat on the hallstand outside, a pair of espadrilles, enough to cover her modesty. There was no money in the handbag, nowhere to go, but none of that mattered, not any longer. All they had to do was get out, knock at the next-door house, hammer as long as it took for one of the inmates to answer, didn't matter if they were resentful. Nobody would listen, but someone had to listen. Perhaps she could encourage response by yelling "Police" through the letter box, or ask Jeanetta to create one of her truly piercing screams, but they were wasting time. Katherine watched: Jeanetta shoveling a small portion of cornflakes in so tidy a fashion she was clearly cured of the habit of mashing all food to pulp, one thin arm transferring the spoon to her mouth with well-mannered speed as if she had only just realized this was the most efficient way to consume, eyeing her mother over the bowl. Slowly, darling, please. Katherine wanted to stop the eating process, flee the house without delay, but she did not have the heart to curtail a tiny meal.

In the mind's frantic calculations lay the knowledge that in real terms, the child had been subsisting on crumbs. She had been on the verge of lunacy, distracted, out of her mind, thinking all the time that it was herself who was the most vulnerable. For a brief moment, she felt as strong as a lion.

"More, Mummy. Please." Dear God, the manners were perfect. So was the obedience.

"No, darling, not yet. We're going now."

"Where?"

"Mrs. Harrison."

"Ohhh, yes." There was a long sigh of sheer relief. Jeanetta had been kneeling on the chair, twisted off it and made for the kitchen door. "I'm bringing Jack."

"Wait. Got to be very, very quiet." Oh why had she mentioned a destination causing this noisy excitement, when all the time the front door was locked, how could she have forgotten? "Come back, darling, come back, not that way. By the window." Katherine's head was clearer than it had ever been, her words showing no shadow of the usual hesitation. Jeanetta obeyed her.

The kitchen window, security locked, but not with a key. On either side the window was fastened against intruders by bolts in the frame, easily unscrewed from the inside. What had once been a steep basement well a few feet below had been boarded over by David to save it being filled with litter from passersby, strong enough boards for a safe landing even if they jumped. They were both such light people. Sudden movements, she noticed, made Jeanetta stagger, issue her polite little cough: her small feet unsteady as she smothered the sound, while Katherine was finding yet more energy, removing the bolts with deft fingers. She had cleaned the inside of the glass yesterday morning, noted the position of the locks even then, but as she opened the sash window, her eyes registered another problem. Once out on the boards above the basement, they would still have to surmount the railings, but all would be possible once they had placed both feet into the outside world. Pad the top of the railings, climb over.

"Sweetheart, fetch one of the dresses from the playroom."

"No, Mummy, please: You go." Jeanetta could not bear to retreat back in that direction. Katherine smiled at her, ran back across

the floor, pulled out the red cloak from the pile of clothes on the floor, ran back, forgetting now the need for shoes or coat, she would do as she was rather than risk opening the door into the hall. "I'll go out first, darling, then you can land on me. Jack will manage." Jeanetta smiled weakly, her face strained.

The stone window ledge barked Katherine's shins and the height of the ledge from the boards was greater than she had imagined. At first she tried to lever herself down, then she jumped, still carrying the red cloak, landed with a thud and a searing pain in one foot. Hurriedly she threw the cape over the railings, turned back to the window. "Jeanetta?" a loud whisper, full of exhilaration. "Come on, darling, quickly." There was silence. No small head appeared above the window, no sign, no voice. The rustling of the fine trees in the street was deafening, the sluggish breeze in the air deliciously cool after the confines of the house. I'm wrong, I'm wrong, Katherine thinking, all wrong, suddenly quite terrified of the dark: I could have simply taken her out through the garden, over the wall at the back, into next door, we could have waited there, just as we were, until morning. She looked briefly at the railings which surrounded her, the height of her shoulder, huge, but not insurmountable. Then called again, "Come on, Jeanetta, come quick, just climb over, I'll catch you. Don't be frightened." There was more silence. Katherine gripped the stone ledge, jumped up to look into the kitchen, saw nothing but the yawning gap of window, unable to see far into the room. Had child gone back for food perhaps? For Jack? Katherine stood irresolute, ready to risk a shout, or climb in again to fetch her daughter, and standing, was aware of a prickling in the scalp. As she held on to the ledge, ready to go back upward, swearing under her breath, she turned her head to one side, stopped. The front door of the house was standing open. David lounged on the top step, shaking his head. He held in his hand the old key to the gate in the railings, and the new key to the door of the house.

"Are you looking for burglars?" he asked. "Or were they looking for you?"

Her headband fluttered to the floor. As if it had controlled the inside of her skull, something in her mind snapped and darkness closed around her.

* * *

Sophie Allendale had always known it would happen someday, and now it had. To her own surprise, she had been the soul of calm, but then she had not caught them in action. The other fears set in later. Her life for the last few years had been geared to fear of this breed, burglars, that was: people she always envisaged from her local paper as being large, fat, working in gangs armed with axes, the scourge of anyone over sixty, all hell-bent on pursuit of her possessions. But she had been talked out of the usual vigilance by one of her friends, who said you can only die once, and the way you carry on, death will be from heatstroke. Don't be so silly-billy, Sophie, Mary Fox had added cozily; even burglars get lazy in the heatwave like this and you'll shrivel up if you don't open the windows. They had been eating tea the other day, or at least, Sophie eating, Mary pacing up and down in an irritating manner, bitching about her sister and also about the heat. Today is August, Granny, do open the windows, there's a dear: having them shut all the time is bad for your skin. This last remark was the deciding factor. Sophie considered her own skin quite remarkable for her age, while Mary considered the panoply of pots necessary to sustain the bloom quite excessive. They prevented access to the bathroom basin. So Sophie, if only to justify the expense of the pots and lotions, had opened the French windows of her living room to find the effect such a relief she forgot to close them again as often as not. Somehow the burglars, or the survival of her furniture, or the prospect of rape, were not as important as they had been and the neurosis of a lifetime slipped sideways. She had other things on her mind.

Such as being barred from the house of son and grandchildren. Distressing was not an adequate word to describe the sense of rejection. She could not begin to explain herself to the coven when she met them for coffee in Luigi's; could find no formula to reply to the question "And how's the lovely babies, then?" without the lie or the equally telling lack of detail becoming transparent. None of them was born yesterday: they relished family conflict and So-phie had lorded over them a little too long. "Wonderful," she would say. "Growing so tall, eating so much," none of this news anything compared to the fulsome details she was accustomed to provide even though her contact with son and grandchildren had never been as frequent or consistent as she had pretended. No

contact at all was not a difference of degree; more like a body blow which left her wheezing and gasping for air, a humiliation so acute she could not mention it. Mary said Katherine was to blame, and although Sophie had not been strictly truthful in her account of the last evening's babysitting, she tended to agree, since it was, in the last analysis, Katherine who had barred her from the house.

When the burglars struck, she had been wandering in a street, which street mattered not, provided there were shop windows and nothing was far from home. She liked looking at antiques if there were any to be seen and was particularly fond of masquerading as a buyer, well aware that her general appearance, her clipped accent and the deceptive appearance of being a lady of means, instead of one who had had her pocket money regulated by her son since ever he was twelve, made the sellers inclined to listen and answer questions for twenty minutes at a time. She was look-ing, vaguely, for pieces of furniture she had once possessed and lost, little tables, chairs, all gone, sold or taken; she had been looking for years, never finding. But in one of these delightful interludes, so frequent now, when she felt the need to chat was even greater than the need to eat, the burglars had found the living room and stepped through it. Unnecessary, she thought, to break one pane of glass: the window was open already.

Oh what a mess. Dearie, dearie me. The room was always one kind of mess in the form of clutter, but this was a different type of mess. She did not find the fact of only the minimum of things being missing to be any sort of comfort. In the course of removing one precious television, a radio not quite so indispensable and two or three ornaments which happened to be recognizably silver, they had invaded every drawer, every cupboard, despite the flimsy locks which Sophie used for the safekeeping of almost everything she owned. The contents appeared to have been tipped on the living-room floor. Looking with quick, birdlike eyes at what was left, Sophie knew a feeling of pique. How dare they imagine that her Staffordshire dogs, her ornaments, the cups of David's which were nickel, not silver, or the lace antimacassars were not worth the bother of stealing? Cheek, ignorant pigs, the indignation soared through her, granting a feeling of superiority which arrested the cold sensation for a minute. She supposed she could call the police,

but only wanted to call her son, and in the dilemma of what to do next, she sat on the floor once she had established there was no one left in the flat and the windows were firmly closed, made tea and began to examine the piles of things on the carpet. No, she would not call the police; she had enough to do with them once, great big brutes. There on the floor was Daddy's death certificate, medical reports citing malnutrition. Oh, he had been so fat and fair once. Fractured skull from falling downstairs, falling, it said. Everything scattered about now, along with his indictment for embezzlement and fraud, his convictions for theft. Sophie shuffled away papers, merely examined the objects, preferring to find things the existence of which she had forgotten. The forced, slow turning over of items which had been locked away was a voyage of discovery, accompanied by a great jumble of memories and confusions, all far more disturbing than the burglars themselves.

For a start, there she had been for something like weeks, ever since her banishment, hating her daughter-in-law with the sort of poisonous hatred which would have made her stick pins in her wax effigy if only she could have found the wax and the hair she believed necessary, but here, on the floor, released from some place of safekeeping, were all those lovely things Katherine had given her in the past. Yes, she pictured it now, this same flat when son David was courting, bless him, that gorgeous girl arriving armed with flowers, chocolates, assorted goodies, clothes. Oh and a care in the choices too, a pink silk scarf so precious that Sophie saved it only for best until she forgot where she had put it, then, saucy girl, some camiknickers which had been the most flattering thing of all, a recognition of being not just any old woman, but a pretty old woman, you know, the age usually the recipient of beastly thermal underwear, delighted to receive something fit for a sexy lady. Sophie had saved those to look at, tried them on sometimes, giggled and decided that she did not dare, but in looking at them now, remembered she had worn the frilly blouses and used the exquisite lace handkerchiefs provided from the same source, and not with David's money either, not as far as she knew, no definitely not. David had been as surprised by the perspicacity of the choices, even a little annoyed, so he certainly had not paid. Oh dearie, dearie me, oh my ears and whiskers. Sophie was scratching at her head, feeling the curls damp with the heat, Katherine even used

to take me to the hairdresser. Katherine loved me, she really did. Whatever Mary says.

The evening had come down like a curtain over a short act, surprising her into dusk. Suddenly she was too exhausted to bother with anything and what did it matter, none of all this had anything to do with Daddy. Tomorrow would do. Nor could she cope with any one of the coven, or Katherine's sister, who would have come round like a shot at the merest hint of disaster. It was only after she went to bed, leaving the mess, only shutting the drawers in the bedroom so as not to be alarmed by different shadows on the walls, that she began to shake and imagine whoever they were would come back. Despite the metal grilles across the broken window frame, piece of nothing to such a team. She could not envisage this as the work of one teenage boy (which it was), lay there quaking and listening for any sound not instantly familiar, got up to fetch the radio at midnight before she remembered it had gone. She made tea, drifted to and fro to the lavatory and sat there for an hour, the bathroom feeling secure since it appeared to have escaped invasion, ah there was a trick to recall for the future, put the silver in there. She tried to think of insurance, the bonus of money back on what was stolen, but could not think straight. All the time she wanted to call her son, strangely wanted to call Katherine. Pride forbade, but she could not stop the wish. Then a squirt of anger intervened. This is my son, my only son: she is my daughter-in-law. I am an old lady. Why the devil does it matter if I call in the middle of the night? At 2:00 A.M., according to the clock too old to be worth the burglars' appropriation, she dialed, but put down the phone after three rings. She imagined it, by the side of their marital bed, oh no, supposing Katherine did not love her after all, put down the phone as soon as someone at the other end picked up their receiver. Then the anger took hold after yet more tea. She dialed again at three. This time she waited for an answer.

Sophie, hand shaking on one end of the telephone, waiting to speak to a son while hoping the spouse of the son would answer. David had been wrong: Katherine would not mind the mess, Katherine never had. Sophie, receiving, after a very long pause, how many rings, she lost track, determined this time to hang on to the receiver as if it were a lifeline, a voice out of the wilderness. David, speaking with a suspicion in his tone which sounded a little like

guilt. "Hallo . . . Who's that?" Not the aggression she might have expected.

"Mummy," she mumbled.

There was an exclamation. "Mummy who?"

"Your mother," Sophie yelled, angry with him for sounding such a stranger.

"Oh."

"You took long enough to answer. What on earth do you think you were doing? I hope you weren't having a nightmare."

"I'm not doing anything, but I was trying to sleep. It's the middle of the night. What do you want, Mother, are you drunk?"

"I've been burgled."

"When? Now?"

She was aware she might achieve more by exaggeration of both timing and scale, but could not bring herself to lie.

"No, this afternoon."

"Did you call the police?"

"Well, no."

"Are you all right?" The question sounded bored.

"Sound in mind and limb if that's what you mean. I only needed to talk. Could I speak to Katherine?" The hesitation was palpable.

"No, you can't: she's asleep. And she hasn't been well."

"I'm sure she won't mind if you ask her. I'm not very well either, as it happens."

He laughed, a little uncertainly. "Not like Katherine, Mama. Different kind of sickness. We think she may be pregnant. Not sure yet."

"Ohhhh!" All Sophie's fears, angers and alarms melted in the face of one sensation of delight. The burglars were forgotten in David's master stroke. Surely her son would need her now. "Ohhh, darling David, you are so clever . . . Ohh, I'll leave her in peace."

"Listen, Ma, it's 3:00 A.M. I can't come over now and leave the children. I'll drift across in the morning."

"You're forty in a few days," Sophie remarked in one of her non sequiturs which only meant she was not anxious to relinquish the phone.

"I know, Mother, I know. Go back to sleep."

She was completely mollified, suddenly weary. "I haven't been

to sleep, oh all right then, sleep tight. Give Katherine a kiss for me. Bye-bye.''

David replaced the phone on the bedside table. The mattress beside him was empty. He was marginally grateful to his mother for the earlier interruption, not for the later. His house was now secure, because of her, all his possessions safely housed. Jeremy slept; there was never such a sleeper as Jeremy. Jeanetta was back where she belonged, out of earshot, while he could imagine the faint sounds of Katherine in the attic, walking up and down, down and up, her frantic rattling of the lock suspended now. She should have known better: such a pity she always had to be taught all over again just as soon as she appeared to have learned. As he drifted into sleep, he remembered the red cloak still on the railings outside and reminded himself to remove it in the morning.

So many tasks.

16

"Do you love me?" My husband asked me that, once, in another life, two years ago.

"Don't be so damned stupid. Go to sleep."

Something like that, was what I said, something derisory. I remembered, wide awake somewhere about four o'clock this morning, and into these ghastly hours comes every single depressing thought, everything I never wanted to know or think, conclusions I have never made.

Then there's a count of everything drunk the evening before in a vain attempt to prove that these broken slumbers and the consumption of alcohol are not related, a piece of mathematics which invariably fails after three gins, half-bottle wine, three more of the same . . . Not much, not much at all, of course not, the old lie turning into that sickly sweet taste in the mouth which tells the truth and makes water into nectar. Sometimes, the deepest sleep follows the waking, but in the small hours, I admit defeat and I miss him. The warm back mostly, the shreds of conversation. The brief intrusion from the front. Did you love me, did you ever love me?

He wasn't always so perfunctory, you see. It was me who started the rot. Bored, grumpy, can't be bothered to go out and I hate this

house, pushing him off while thinking instead of sums or clients and taxes, ignoring the children the way I had been, ever so nicely, ignored. Such a tidy house of servants, the one of my childhood and the one I created, no responsibilities for Mother. Perhaps privilege does this, I do not know, made me so frightened of intimacy through lack of practice, keeping life as formal as possible, but I begin to see how modern man wants more, suffering the same as us from a rising of expectations. They want cuddles and a warm kitchen as well as brain; want us to civilize them with talk, comfort and wallpaper so that pure marriages of equal minds and equal duties may not work. Mine was always treated like a deal, Sebastian and I like directors on the board and if we disagreed, he was outvoted. Less said the better, mine was the only way, never a hint of democracy here and precious little sentiment either. Something there was I missed or I would not be missing him now. Would not consider, in the purgatory of the early morning, begging him to come back, and if pride was once my backbone, it has a curvature. In my own loneliness, I now see, his.

Backache, heartache, headache. Yesterday morning I had all three as well as the peculiar conviction of being woken by something other than the pre-dawn nausea, opted for pillow over head until daylight, gave up toward six and wobbled toward the study for some pretense at work. And God, the heat. Weeks of this constant sweat, making everything gray, an open window carrying the mockery of a breeze as fetid as a cow's breath, the air so thick you could cut it with a knife. Not a sound in the street when I look out to check if anything else is alive, blinking downward to something like a flag on the railings flanking the Allendales' house, so startling I squint and look again, very quietly. Thick red material on top of the blunt spikes near the front window, a sort of red carpet for a burglar's bottom. Pretty and pretty odd: half asleep, I tried harder for the imperfect view which misses their front windows and the recess of the door, nothing visible, no sight or sound apart from the red material, hanging there like a signal while I feel absurdly disappointed to see nothing more malicious.

They weigh on one now, if you can understand, a family like that, so bloody self-contained, and they treat me as if I did not exist, the first humiliators of the deserted wife. I can't approach them, knowing what I know, but I wanted one of them to approach

me with the hand of friendship we're supposed to have, but neither of them will. To think I liked them once after my own fashion while now I tend to despise them for despising me: you would think their children had never spent the greater part of two years in my house because in the few weeks since they left, there's been scarcely a word. Oh I know David gave Mrs. Harrison a large sweetener, but it doesn't follow that the kids should have disappeared so completely. Mark may have found Jeanetta a pain, but now he sulks, so does Samantha. They are a little confused by the absence of Daddy, however little they saw of him: having those Allendale brutes around the place would have helped since what seems to control children most is the presence of other children. Oh damn, damn, damn. All right, Sebastian, you've made your point. I can't bring myself to call you darling, but okay, you did help: you actually did far more than I, and I miss you.

Did you love me, my husband? Did I try? It was me, wasn't it? And you in spirit, sitting on that park bench, lonely as a day in hell.

I shouted last time we met, but my heart wasn't in the noise I was making and when he had his turn he spoke with more authority than I'd ever remembered. He has fine eyes and his hair was untidy, I wanted to touch while I capitulated so much, thought so much, realizing things I never knew, and if suffering ennobles the human spirit, I would prefer to remain base. There is no black and white to life anymore, only shades of gray like dirty washing. He looked leaner and fitter, which irked me into the shouting and also drinking more, watching him watch me and seeing through his eyes what it did to my speech. Oh for the luxury of drunkenness instead of the confusion, the vulgar cracks, occasional obscenities and sharp memory for irrelevant jokes which float to the surface of my wine, making me less and less able to get what I want. As if I knew any longer what that was. I drink therefore I digress, and in that process, acceded to all demands. The end-result is that later this evening, Sebastian will come to the door and take Mark away for a couple of days. They will have their own holiday while my spouse and I continue to deliberate, ha, ha. The men of the household seem to be winning.

On that dull thought I was finishing his packing, most of it done

by Mrs. Harrison since I do not even know where my children keep their clothes. Such miniature things for a miniature Sebastian, me putting them in a bag and wanting him to come in and say he preferred my company to his father's but knowing he wouldn't, and wishing I did not deserve it; when in the middle of what threatened to be tears, Mrs. Harrison, more tight-lipped these days than ever, came to see if I was in control. Not of myself, of the packing. And also to "have a word." Her presence was an unwelcome echo of my own redundancy: "a word" is never brief and she never chooses the right time. I wanted Sebastian to come and go: I did not want to listen.

"Mrs. Pearson," she said, picking things up and putting them down, "Mr. Harrison suggested I have a word . . ."

"What's the matter with him, cat got his tongue?" She ignored that. Harrison is a man of few words.

"About next door," she said firmly. I remembered the red flag on the railings, remembered at the same time that the silence with our neighbors would soon have to be breached. David Allendale's birthday party. Social obligation, sometime soon.

She cleared her throat. "Mrs. Pearson, have you seen Jeanetta? I mean, anywhere? Only I got to wondering if Mrs. Allendale had been in to see you. When we was busy, that is. Recently, I mean. Some evening, perhaps? Maybe said how she was." The voice trailed away. She knows very well that no one comes into this house without her knowledge, noted by her eagle eye and their dimensions measured. Or lack of dimensions, in Katherine's case.

"No, not either of them." (Not as far as I know: the days are so blurred.) "Oh, yes, I have. No, wait a minute. I've seen her going out, both of them. And him coming in. With Jeremy. Yes I've seen them all. I think."

She sagged with relief. "Are you sure, the little girl, I mean, Jeanetta?" standing there, doggedly persistent in the face of indifferent replies.

"No, not completely sure. Why the hell does it matter?"

"I'm worried about her," said Mrs. Harrison, limp before bursting forth again. "I mean, very worried. Nothing. Not a word. She's just gone. You can't keep a child in a street like this and make it invisible. S'posing she's sick or something? I've knocked and said

I'll take her out and he says she's out already, thank you, but why don't I ever see her go? Don't even ask me to babysit like they used. You'd have thought . . .''

"You mustn't spy on them. They're none of our business. Can't you see they're probably keeping out of the way because of that business with the necklace?'' I was stuffing a toy inside Mark's kit with all my strength. She flapped her hands, running short of words, looking anguished, opening her mouth but not speaking. Then Mark sidled into the room, peeped from behind her back. I could sense in him a desire to be gone, wanting these few days with his father as a woman might crave diamonds or a lover, impatient desire written all over him, and so hurtful it took away my breath, but I could see I had not devoted enough to him to warrant anything more. But all the same, the harshness of the ache made me angry with him. In retrospect, I was at my worst.

"I seen her,'' he said. "Me and Sammy saw.''

"Who?'' All so irrelevant I'd forgotten already, Katherine, Jeanetta, indifferent to both, my eyes on my son. "Where?'' said Mrs. Harrison, pouncing on him, holding his shoulders. This annoyed me more. Unhand my son who does not touch me, afraid I might spoil his treat. He twisted, shrugged her off, sure indication of something shameful. They had secrets, those two.

"In the garden,'' he muttered finally. "Dreaming.''

Mrs. H took him by the arms again: he was frightened, but I didn't know why, her yelling and I didn't know why either. "What do you mean, dreaming? And how did you see? When? You been poking in their garden, have you? How d'you get in? I've told you not to climb that wall at the end, it isn't safe . . .''

I said, yes, yes, automatically. She glared at me and we both waited for Mark. Watched him put on his best mulish and defensive face like his father, thinking of the imminence of Daddy and wanting to avoid trouble.

"Sitting on the steps. Their steps. You can just see, only just, from the bottom. I was looking for puss, she's been sick again. I put my head through the fence thing.'' He meant the trellis with the half-dead creeper.

"Talk to her?'' Mrs. Harrison barked. "What's she look like then?''

He kicked the floor, pawing the carpet with his feet, sulking and

anxious. "She was dreaming," he repeated. "She didn't take any notice when I shouted at her. Sitting on those steps what go up to their kitchen, I think."

"Which go up to their kitchen," I said.

The interruption made him hurry. Mrs. Harrison added hers, angry. "Was she playing then, was she? What was she doing? And how long since?"

He wrinkled his forehead. "Oh, a day or two. Or three or four, I don't know, don't look at me like that . . . Oh, when's Daddy coming? All right then, I shouted at her, hallo or something, but she wouldn't listen or didn't hear, didn't want to. I thought she was being snotty. Just sitting there in the sun, on the steps, wearing this funny long dress all over. Singing. Only for a minute. Then her daddy came out and she stopped and I went aways. He doesn't like peoples in his garden. Or looking at him."

"Sounds perfectly fine," I said crossly. "Dressing up again. Always was fond of other people's clothes, that girl." He shook his head, wanting to say something more, not daring.

"Mrs. Pearson," said our Mrs. Harrison, sizing up to me like a fighter with her fists clenched. "Mrs. Pearson . . . ma'am, the reason I'm mentioning this is 'cause Samantha saw Jeanetta, last week, I think, she doesn't really know, you know how vague she is. These scamps," she gestured to Mark, who blushed, "have been trying to get in next door. Their own garden not good enough, see. Only Sam says Jeanetta was poorly. Not like she was, you know, not fat anymore. Says she was as thin as a lizard. Like a little rat. It's no good, Mrs. Pearson, you've just got to go and ask what's happened to her. I can't: I've tried. Something's gone wrong. You've got to go. When will you go?"

"Well, things never go wrong singly, do they?" It was the tone of the order in her voice which hit that large part of me already primed with a sort of grief, anger, disappointment, Mark, Sebastian, sleepless nights of new recrimination, and terrible dawns. I had nothing left, not even the authority of the mistress of the house, standing there, receiving commands while I listen to these blatant and alarmist exaggerations. Blood rose in my face: she stepped away from me, spontaneous regret, and into that tiny vacuum of silence, the doorbell rang. Mark dashed past us both, hurling himself downstairs, yelling, "Daddy, Daddy, Daddy," leaving me and

the rebellious servant, both with a hand on the half-closed case. My son would have gone naked with his father, and that was all I knew. I regretted it while almost understanding in one fell moment, greater than other regrets, blotting out anything more. Had I wept in her arms, Mrs. Harrison might have liked me, but I did not, could not. Instead I followed downstairs, found Mark struggling with the door like a demented animal, only partially calmed by Harrison, who opened with the butler's dignity, a smile on his face.

I never saw it before, only dreamed it now in the wake of the dawns, the love Sebastian inspires in anyone else. Without counting the days since he left, I know how long they have been, how rudderless the household, how genuine that great grin of pleasure on Harrison's face. I never knew, I never knew, and ignorance was bliss in the old arrogance of never caring. They all adore him. He was framed in the doorway, a handsome man for all that, whose life I have left as a blank, never asking what he did with it or wanted to do. Apart from keep me in the style I could afford, cater for my carelessness and stay away when the drunken going was rough. He did not come in: I mounted the stairs, becoming the servant, to fetch the incomplete bag belonging to the son, carried it down with me, handed them over to one another as if neither had ever been mine, smiling, smiling, smiling. Not in front of the children. No weeping please. Nothing, but wishing well. Seeing my failures. Furious, impotent, sadder than age, weak at the knees. Smiling. Have fun, Oh, when are you coming back? I don't suppose, no, no, never mind. "What was it?" he asked, Sebastian speaking, holding Mark by the hand. I kicked the carpet on the floor, the same way Mark kicks carpet to hide embarrassment. "We . . . ell nothing. The Allendales' party . . . will you be back?" He has a memory for dates which is like an instinct, the same, I remember, as the instinct which never wanted to hurt. "Of course," he said. "Not long, is it? Perhaps we'll go?" "Please," I said. "We'll be back, won't we?" Mark looked up. "I suppose so." He took his turn at kicking the carpet. "Don't do that, Mark," I said, wishing I had not spoken. "All right. See you."

I can't remember who closed the door.

There was worse, of course. There is always worse whenever you think you've hit the bottom. Such as Samantha flying down-

stairs in her nightie, a ghost with a red and angry face. A mistake perhaps to keep the fleeting visit of her father such a secret: I was consulted on the subject, could not remember. Think I said we could do without both the jealousy or excitement. Thinking her turn would come, if I thought at all. We might as well not have bothered: the decision was not good. Democracy applies to children too. "Was Daddy," she shrieked. "Daddy. I heard him, I did, I did, I did . . ."

"Come on, sweetheart: back to bed. Late," said Mrs. Harrison grimly. Samantha turned to me. She is like me in so many ways while Mark resembles his father. Samantha has none of their mildness, a will of iron and a foghorn voice.

"You didn't tell me. Was Daddy, it was . . ." No one denied it. ". . . You didn't tell me. You never said he was coming here. I want Daddy. Daddy, Daddy, Daddy . . ."

"All right, all right," I moved to touch her, watched her leap away from my infection. "Why?" she wailed. "Why?"

"Because . . ."

"I hate you, Mummy. Piggy, piggy cow. Bastard, bottoms." Oh where do they get the words? She stood there trembling, the little face contorted with tears of fury, the whole of her concentrated on producing the worst insult she could summons, the most hurtful thing she could imagine.

"Fat legs!" finally spat from her. "Big bums. Stupid ole witch. Hate you."

Laughable, yes, this pocket-battleship rage, comic in any other set of eyes but mine. She fled upstairs, unnerved by her own hysteria, sobbing. Even without energy, I should have followed, but the stiff upper lip was well in place, not selfishness exactly, only guilt. So instead, Mrs. Harrison went after her and knew she would be the most welcome.

Drink, drink, drink. Not in the kitchen, Harrisons have eyes, melting into the back of their bloody heads when they go downstairs, X-ray eyes like antennae. Confused: now what exactly do I want, bottles hugged to bosom, still clanking up the stairs. Tonic for the gin supply hidden in the study desk. Somewhere, long after ten o'clock, I was aware of Harrison's deferential knock at the door. And did not answer. Even later, the pinging of the phone. The servants, using the line downstairs, running my house. I went

to sleep in the chair. Finally, in the dawn, I cried. For the mess I had made.

Please help me, please. I want to do better: I have learned so much too quickly and I did not see. There is nothing more salutary than being left alone. More than anything else, I want all those children back. So I can start again.

17

"I DON'T BELIEVE YOU. YOU'VE LOST YOUR MIND TO DO SUCH A THING . . . How did you do such a thing?"

"Easy enough. Don't know really. But it won't last, I shouldn't worry. He more or less said so, and I agreed. Besides, it simply isn't practical. Fun though." At the moment, Monica did not look entirely sure. Jenny thought she looked more dispirited than illuminated. The whole effect was disappointing.

"Practical? Never mind practical, it isn't fair either," she spluttered. "In fact, completely unfair. How would you feel, oh, sorry, I forgot you sort of know how it feels, but poor Katherine. You shouldn't, not to a friend. For Christ's sake we were all going to their party next week: I won't know where to put my face."

"You won't know? What about me?"

"If you go," said Jenny rudely, "that'll be your problem. Mess on your own doorstep and then you have to clean up. Or at least sidestep. Colin will notice. You can't go."

"Yes I shall go and no, he won't notice. Don't be such a prig for God's sake. Besides you're forgetting she messed first. Ogling my husband as if men were newly invented . . ."

"But she didn't, Monica, not exactly. I'm sorry, but I thought it was the other way around."

"I don't care which way round it started. He still got a chest full of lipstick, cigarettes crunched in his back pocket, grass bits in the turn-ups of his trendy trousers. Loves the great outdoors, but you don't collect that kind of litter without an element of participation. Don't pity Katherine. Not the first time. Past master at the game. Mistress, I mean." The voice was suddenly vicious.

"Oh I don't think so, surely not. She'd be too . . ."

"Well, he told me so himself, David, I mean. David told me lots and lots about Katherine. She's a slut. Paternity of one child seriously in doubt. Always the quiet ones, isn't it?" They were sitting in Jenny's garden. Monica drew on her cigarette and threw away the end so the lit stub glowed for a full minute on the lawn. Jenny was silent. None of this equated with her own experience of a sheltered life and she was not sure quite what she believed. On several occasions in a long acquaintance, Monica had been careless with the truth, creating exaggerations. Jenny bracketed this last news along with similar examples of the same syndrome and refrained from comment. Katherine had been weighing on her conscience, lightly but unaccountably, and although she would have liked some scandal to prove Katherine was horrid and absolve herself from that niggling guilt, Monica's revelations were not providing any such reassurance. Rather the opposite, and, on the underside of disgust at the bad behavior of a friend, there was a prurient curiosity yearning to be satisfied. Hardly a moral question, but what did he do, she wanted to know: exactly how did he get you into bed or on to the floor, feet first or what? And what did he do next? Give me the details, please, without me having to ask. Instead, she sidestepped.

"I don't understand," she said slowly. "Not quite, anyway. You spent the whole afternoon at their house, but where the hell were the rest of them, such as Katherine and the kids?"

Monica stretched and yawned. Jenny caught a whiff of fresh perfume from one exposed underarm, was embarrassed. Did people wash after such adulterous assignations? She supposed they did.

"Katherine was out. Always out whenever she can, gym or some such self-indulgent thing, such as spending the hard-earned cash: how awful, our conservatory might go to pay for her clothes. Probably creating or preserving the body beautiful. I wonder why

he liked mine? No real comparison, is there?" She made an attempt
to laugh which was far from the usual full-bellied sound. "Anyway,
Jeremy, the boy, he'd been left at some playschool David's found,
sort of trial run for the afternoon, and Jeanetta wasn't there. Empty
house. Perfect." She paused, reached for the wine on the table
between them, frowned. "Well, he said it was an empty house.
No disturbances, no knocks, no tradesmen at the door, but when
we were upstairs, in his studio place—no, not their bedroom, he
didn't suggest it and I couldn't have done it—I kept feeling as if
someone was there."

"Ghosts. Or conscience," Jenny snorted. "Serve you right."
Monica shrugged. "Probably. There were sounds from the attic,
or at least I think it was the attic. Above the studio, something
like a mouse or a cat creeping round. I mentioned it and he laughed
at me, said it was nothing if not birds in the roof space. The rooms
above us were always empty. We'll go and look if you like, he
said, but I said no. I didn't want to creep around her house more
than I needed. I'm not quite a natural for this game, you see."
She shivered and reached for the multicolored cardigan on the
back of her chair.

"Monica," said Jenny, "tell me something . . . Is he . . . is he a
fantastic lover? Is that what it is?"

Monica fiddled with the buttons on the dreamcoat. She could
not have worn such a comfortable garment to any meeting with
David because she knew he would never have liked it. Too bright
and fussy. Looking for these small compensations, she paused,
considering the question.

"Yes, he is as a matter of fact. Very strong, very dominant . . .
All male. Doesn't ask, but knows what to do. Knows where everything is. If you see what I mean." Jenny saw perfectly well.

"And is it worth it? On that account?"

"No," said Monica, hugging her arms to her chest and fingering
a small bruise below the sleeve of the dreamcoat. "No, I don't
really think it is." She turned to Jenny, her face flushed. "Which
is why we've all got to go to this party and you've got to help me.
There's only a few others; we've got to go. It's quite all right, Jenny
darling, the whole little escapade has finished. If I don't finish it,
he will. He loves his life and he loves Katherine, you see. Loves
everything in his house too much to risk a thing. So we'll go on,

all of us, just as we did before, as if nothing ever happened. Like real grown-ups." Her eyes were shining, tears or determination Jenny could not tell in her own sensation of acute relief. She felt inclined to keep the conversation neutral.

"In that case, I'll do what I was going to do anyway. Because I was a bit worried about her. Have the kids over to play with ours one weekend. This weekend. Give Katherine a break."

Sympathy for Katherine was still not what Monica wanted to hear. "Count me out. You can try, though. I seem to remember him saying Jeanetta was going to stay with her granny. Or she's already gone. If you want to be useful, you'd better check first. I think we need another bottle of wine."

His footsteps came upstairs soon after midnight. He was trotting noisily on the last, uncarpeted flight, his leather mules clicking on the wood. "When I've made a sitting room up here," he had once told her, "I want green carpet up these steps, with brass stair rods to catch the light and show off the wood. Nice." He had looked at the stairs with the satisfaction he reserved for new territory waiting to be tamed. "There's a fortune in attics," he had added. "All that space, hidden away."

Hidden away in the attic room at the back for over twenty hours, Katherine had stopped counting time since late afternoon. Pieces of her watch lay on the floor from her efforts to concentrate her mind and hands by taking the thing apart with the aid of a hair-slide and a nail which had worked up from the floorboards. Destroying any knowledge of time seemed important. He had showed her in there with her one plastic bowl and a thin blanket: the bowl smelled in the corner and the blanket was damp with sweat, although she had only covered herself briefly since the night before. That was in the afternoon, when she tried to smother the sounds she had heard from the room below.

Long before that, after the key first turned, she had deafened herself with her own screaming. Hitting the door, pounding the lock and screaming for Jeanetta. Put her with me, David, please, please, please, until the voice had trailed into a dry shout, coughing the way the child had coughed, the futility of such racket painfully obvious. Something returned; a remnant of the realism which had got her out of the kitchen window to escape, shoved back down

into the recesses of logical thought because she could no longer afford logical conclusions. Such as the fact that no one could hear unless they were David, who could sleep through a storm and did not wish to respond. Exhaustion won, so she slept herself in a crazed kind of way, dozing into nightmares as the shadows of the moon through the high window danced in the corners and grew enormous. They were static, but moved when she watched them, black figures advancing until she whimpered against the wall.

He had been so cunning, doing this. David knew her weakness, knew very well her horrors, the imprisonments and escapes of the past. Katherine counted on her fingers all the times she had ever been locked away. That time with Mary, when they were found in the coal hole and given flannel pajamas: then another time with foster parents, not in the dark, a benign punishment for bad behavior. Then being told to remain quiet in a room while the favorite foster parent died, or being shut in a room to defray the amorous attentions of the last borrowed daddy of them all, before return to the hostel with the rigid curfew from which Mary had plucked her, still willful, impetuous, high-spirited, into the liberal regime of Mary's bossiness. There was one corollary in all of these imprisonments which loomed largest now. If she was good, without protest, darkness was always followed by light, hugs, apologies, attention, sometimes treats. They were always sorry when they shut you up; so much so there had been a part of her which even grew to like it, see in each episode an anticipation of what would follow. They would expect to see her helpless, cherish her like a baby doll, every time. Being let out was like having a birthday, all over again.

Some dim resentment stirred in the blackness of the attic room. There had been no treats, no being allowed to be a child like that ever since she had given birth to one. It wasn't fair, it was all too much, what about me, me, me?

Somebody hug me, please: I can't cope. Like the aftermath of all those other times, not at his hand. David would be sorry for locking her away. And when he was sorry, he was nice. When he was sorry, she became as precious as a tiny little child. She was loved when he was sorry and she had been good, treated like the fragile crystal they displayed with their food, shining and admirable, touched gently.

Then the shadows touched her skin: she could feel tendrils of darkness stroking her cheek, wrapping themselves around her throat, creeping between her legs, extensions of familiar night-mares, but if she screamed, she would stay here forever. Or as the last alternative, she could be put outside in the dark, where the shadows would become hands, tearing her apart with sharp nails, forcing her to run and run and run. Even in the depths of night-mare, cringing toward the window, she could perceive at least the solidity of the wall behind which shadows could not creep, while the fate beyond the door of the house might be worse. Better in here than out, far better. There was logic in this punishment, not quite the worst she had known since there was still a surface to clutch as darkness paled into light. She remembered what silent obedience brought; embraces, sweeties, kisses, protection. All the bravery of the evening before, the logic, the realism, died. Katherine simply waited and endured, forgetting everything.

Dawn had been short-lived relief as time sped forward, the comfort of light short-lived as the sun rose and eleven o'clock heat raised the room to an oven, so warm she could not have shouted without water. Then, in the middle of her fit of strangled coughing, he had come back, standing clean and polished in the doorway, holding a jug of water. For the liquid, she would have crawled, but she stayed as she was, knees clutched to chest, her fingers twisting her hair with little movements. He put the jug by the door, finger on his lips.

"You've been very naughty. You've got to be good. For a little while." There was a promise in that, the beginnings in him of the guilt for which she watched and hoped, made herself smaller in the belief he would notice. Be good, sweet child, and let who will be clever. So she was good. Monstrously good. Picking up the tiny particles of dust and fluff which dwelt on the floor, rolling the fluff into balls and making a neat, housewifely pile of miniature rubbish. Busy until she heard them in the studio below. Shocked into stillness by Monica's voice, the loud, braying laugh cutting a line through her forehead, the noise of it absorbed through her eyes and skin. Katherine opened her own mouth to shout, remembered, placed one finger over her teeth and bit her knuckle. Don't say a word: don't speak: be good, and something nice will happen. Familiar enough sounds from him: the same noises he had made

so lately without a wall between them, and from the woman, a crescendo of moaning, but Katherine had the blanket over her head and stuck into her ears as she began, stealthily, to dismember her watch. The bracelet was gold. In the daylight hours left, using her teeth, she had prised apart seven of the links. She added them to the little pile of fluff. As long as he came back.

The key turned in the lock and he was framed in the electric light from the hallway, hurrying toward her, pulling her upright and wrapping his arms around her. "Darling, darling, darling . . . I'm sorry. All right now, not your fault, was it?"

She stood limp with her arms by her sides as he embraced, pressing the back of her head into the shoulder which was soft and warm. A river of perspiration ran down into the valley of her bosom, stuck to the nightdress which was grubby from the floor. She had thought that another night would have made her die, but she had waited for this, had known he would be like this. The heat of her body ended in arms icy cold, the rich cashmere of his sweater soothing. He adjusted her arms so they rested around his waist and she left them there, fingers touching lifelessly. Comfort was comfort, nothing registered but the end of the nightmare, the reward.

Downstairs, from the studio, there was a tinkling of music from the radio.

"You must be hungry," he said with infinite gentleness, "poor little thing. A bath first. Then bed. I'll bring you up some supper. Something simple. Glass of wine. You'd like that." She shuddered violently in the return of memory, only semi-free from the mesmerizing darkness, dug her fingers into his haunches, spoke the first words. "Jeanetta. Netta . . . What have you done?"

"Shhh, shhh. Don't worry. All over now."

"What have you done?" The repetition was dry, a voice which had to ask but did not really want to know. Knowing would ruin the treat.

"Taken her to stay with Sophie. She wanted to go. Sophie wanted to have her. Give us a break. Naughty girl, trying to get out. Leading you astray. It's all her fault, you know that, don't you? She's always doing that, making you naughty. No good for the two of us, is she? Always been her, spoils things. Should have been a boy." He stroked the back of her hair, feeling the tangles

made by hours of twisting. "Anyway, she's fine, absolutely fine. They'll be eating biscuits. Sort of holiday. Just you and I, darling. I'll look after you."

"Not my fault," she repeated in a babyish voice. Disinterest in Jeremy was evident, as complete as his in her. Rippling waves of physical relief moved from her feet to her head and she slumped against him, her fingers locking behind his back. She did not ask why this, why the other: she had been schooled for years not to ask why; it did not matter. What mattered was belief in safety, belief in him, flooding back like a tide, washing before it all the scum of incredulity.

"Come downstairs, with me. Just for a minute. I want to show you something."

"What?" Fresh fear gripped her lungs.

"Something."

The elegant stairs seemed to number a hundred steps: she held back, but he nudged her on with one arm around her and guiding her all the way down to the grand front door. Opened it, simply stood there with her in the doorway, both of their feet on the step. The kitchen door was shut on her left and she could hear the comforting sound of the boiler humming in the background. She shivered in the nightdress and pushed her hair behind her ears.

"Listen," he said softly, both of them facing the wide road, "you can go whenever you want. There it is, all yours. Go now, if you like. I'll get you some shoes. And a coat."

Over the road, a chestnut tree stirred into life, rustling and hissing in a warm breeze. The noise was sudden and fierce, announcing a storm. One street lamp shone level with the lowest branches of the tree, twigs smacking against the glass, and a single moth, drawn by the light from their own home, blundered into Katherine's face so she covered her eyes. Apart from the lamp and two lights from the house opposite obscured by heavy curtains, the street was as empty as desert, the heat wave finished. Katherine regarded the view with unspeakable horror, a flood of panic hitting her as her bare feet scratched on the cold step. She leaned back against her husband, felt his warmth, watched as he crushed the moth in one palm. Katherine clung to the other arm and they retreated indoors.

Sleep, after bath, after food. Sleep with her hair sweet and wet from water she wanted to drink. Curled like a fetus, safe. Sleep;

as gorgeous as any hallucination. Fingering a swollen stomach, sleep. Jeanetta with her granny, sleeping both. She had been good and everything was going to be all right.

When John Mills failed to get his award, he began to cry. He knew the failure on the Saturday morning when nothing arrived in the post and a colleague from the NSPCC phoned in anticipation of sharing his own good news. If both had won recognition instead of only one of them, they would have joked and said how ridiculous was the whole idea: as if it mattered, such silly condescension, stick the thing in the lavatory. A certificate and a piece of silver sculpture from a posh shop, only fit to be pawned, but best placed all the same in the bathroom's insulting obscurity where every visitor would be bound to see it. But it did matter. Nothing was any longer all right.

John found these days he cried often and with ease, quickly moved to tears by either affectionate gestures or frustration, but mostly by animals, real ones as well as creatures in pictures. He even considered changing his allegiance away from human beings entirely. The award, however silly, would have been a marker on the last years, made them look worthwhile although he doubted they were, as well as giving him some incentive either to carry on, or retire with laurels. So it mattered, desperately. Matilda found him with three of the kittens on his knee, stroking them one by one while they dug experimental claws into his thighs. He was talking, ostensibly to the animals, really to himself, but in any event the chat was exclusive.

Half of her wished this was madness while the rest of her recognized it was not. Nothing wrong but a man without company and capable of receiving none. Matilda was confused and the confusion floated on top of a cocktail of rage. There was this other man, extending on each of their emotional meetings the invitation of alternative life. A house in the suburbs, not only all paid, but entirely free of cats; even with all the fussiness attached, an attractive prospect. Bugger true love: she'd done all that, but as the delicious specter of such an untried existence grew into sharper prospect, so did the ultimatums. Matilda had determined to abandon her own stinking ship, at some time to coincide with this bloody award: leaving John stronger, but instead of jubilation, she

was here, encountering a husband talking to his cats. Their cats, almost their only common property, symbolizing everything she did not want.

She regarded John with all of herself sinking into despair, looked at the animals with loathing. One of them played with her feet and the impulse to kick it out of the window was almost irresistible.

"Pussy, pussy, pussy: Give daddy a kiss."

The hidden obscenity might have been laughable if she had not overheard John's telephone conversation with the half-known colleague, all that talk conducted in tones of forced jollity, quite different to the voice reserved for cats, a silly, childish voice. She looked at that pale face of sunny gentleness, big hands holding horrible kittens fast growing beyond the reach of a palm. Ignoring the vacancy of his expression, she centered on the animals. John removed them from his knees one by one without ever looking at her, his face alive with concern for the movement of all those flailing little legs. In one awful gulp of a conclusion she knew yet again that she could not leave him here. Not today, even if it was the last chance of several, similar days to this, with her tenure on the alternative weakening with every procrastination.

"I'd better go to work," was all he said.

"Don't," she said, surprised by the sound of her own voice.

"I must."

"No, you mustn't."

"What else should I do?" He did not seek comfort, never sought second opinions or even asked what she might have suggested. He had sprung a lifetime's trap without any kind of permission. Frustration boiled inside her, a quiet, white heat. He never consulted, never even canvassed opinion, and the quiet adoration was not enough.

"Go then," she said turning away. "Enjoy yourself."

He placed all the kittens in the box where Kat slept, a larger box by now, with an even larger and cleaner version waiting to accommodate them tomorrow after the same early morning running up the walls which had woken them that morning. Kittens settled with satisfaction, sucking mother like little pigs although they had already eaten solid food. The cat litter in one enormous tray was fresh, but the scent of urine still lingered.

After the door shut on her departing husband, Matilda com-

pleted the business of dressing. Then walked up and down, her steps going quicker and quicker in the confinement of the small living room. She cried briefly, but reverted to the white anger, hatred for everything about her existence, especially the cowardice and the cats. When the frantic pacing stopped, the stillness of the whole place was unnerving. She pulled on a jacket since the night's rain still chilled the upper stories; found the new cardboard box and inverted it over the kittens' bed. With them imprisoned and her handbag over one shoulder, she lifted the double box and went out of the door, closing it but ignoring the double lock. By the time she carried the large burden downstairs, juggling the load to open the door to the backyard, she was out of breath. She set the box down against the far wall. Next to the heap of old newspaper and the rug which formed the makeshift bed for Rotty the Rottweiler's rump, whenever he arrived. Matilda intended no real harm, did not suspect animals of malice, but it seemed appropriate to put them all together. This would be the first place John would look: he would simply be shocked out of his lethargy and that was the full extent of his wife's conscious desires.

"Quick, quick, Eric. Quick. There's someone outside."
Eileen Harrison panted upstairs. Harrison panted down.
"Quick," hissed Eileen. "Quick, while she's out to the shops, for God's sake."
They pattered back toward basement level. "Sammy, you stay there," Mrs. Harrison ordered. "Just for a minute, good girl." She closed the upstairs kitchen door and Samantha began to howl. "Shut up this minute, you hear me?" The crying stopped. "Eric, it's that little beggar, I'm sure it is. Knocking at our back door. What's the matter with him? I'm frightened, Eric, I am. What's he want, must be mad, isn't he? Mad as a hatter, coming back in here. What the hell . . . ?" They paused in the half-light of the stairwell. The innocence of Saturday morning going on all around them, patter-patter outside, did nothing to alter the tension of conspiracy. The tapping at the door went on. Both of them were panting.
"What if he's come back with that bloody necklace?" Eileen whispered, grabbing Eric's arm.

"Don't be so stupid. He wouldn't do that. No one'd do that, you silly cow."

"What does he want then? He's knocking at our kitchen window as if he was crazy. He's gone nuts." Harrison thought for thirty seconds, the strain puckering his eyebrows.

"Call the police. Quickest way to get rid of him before Mrs. P comes home from the shops. We'll all be for the high jump if anyone knows he's been in here before. Specially me. Can't take being lied to, can she? You know what she's like. About things."

"He'll tell them, and they'll tell her, what's the difference. Get rid of him. He can talk, can't he?"

"Maybe not. So what if he does? Never seen him before in my life, nor anyone else either. Call them buggers, go on. I'll see what he wants. Go on. You can shut her up an' all." Samantha's wails were resumed.

The vagrant had overslept. Huddled in a red cloak, he had waited outside a semi-familiar house for most of the afternoon and then he started to explore, ending up in the park. Drugged by the sun and betrayed by the heat's failure to recede with the light, he remained where he was, dead to the world. So soundly he slept under the bushes, the vigilant parkkeepers did not find him. He slumbered without sound, helped by a quart of cider. Stiffly he sidled out of the park, back toward where his billet was, but he could not remember precisely where to go, sidestepped up and down the right-looking road, disorientated and confused. Everywhere looked the same and everywhere was so black he began to feel giddy. Even equipped with the red cloak he had found over a railing the morning before, he was not equipped for nights and besides, was afraid of the dark. He was superstitious, easily alarmed; and as his friend had noticed, beginning to go a little crazy.

So he wandered manfully up and down, down and up in ever decreasing circles, pausing against parked cars, bored, frightened and wakeful after a long sleep, but still craving the oblivion of more. More than sleep, he needed a place of safety, even one of the hostels if he knew the nearest. About midnight, a police car caught him mid-roadway: the driver slowed the vehicle and looked at him closely. He stuck his nose in the air and began to walk with

exaggerated purpose, half stepping, half running, a comic movement down an alley at the end of a road, as if he knew where he
was going. Once out of sight he scaled a wall far higher than the
scope of his normal efforts, found himself in a small garden, un-
kempt and empty, so empty he felt the opposite of safe, so climbed
another high wall on the opposite side. Reckless by now, he simply
wanted a place to rest where he could see lights and know there
was someone there, even though he planned to have moved long
before they saw him. He wanted to look at lit windows to relieve
his own isolation whatever the risk: the sight of people was better
than empty sky, kept at bay the threatening ghost which had begun
to torture his dreams. By the time he reached the third garden, he
had no choice but staying put since the energy which had driven
him so far so fast died in his skinny chest to the tune of loud
panting and a pain over his heart. In any event, this garden was
nicest on account of lights burning safely in far upstairs windows
of the house to which it belonged. He had settled into a hidden
area beneath elegant steps which he only admired for the shelter
they offered. Put the red cloak around himself and slept without
caring when the rain began to fall.

Sleep proved treacherous for the second time, carrying his oblivion well over dawn and into the hours when life was busy
around him. Cars in the street beyond, a drain gurgling close to
his ear, flies buzzing and the whole world wide awake, tickling
his grubby skin with a very slight awareness of danger. Despite all
that, he still could not find a sense of urgency. Everything about
him was blunt and his feet were wet, nor could he remember the
route he had taken to get where he was. After standing and shaking
himself, he climbed beyond the steps up into the garden, noticing
the blank French windows and on one side a projecting wall with
a narrow window at his own head height. Something drew him
to the cozy little window, jammed open for a crack at the top,
familiar temptation of a man who was not really a thief, but still
an opportunist, reassured by the silence of the building despite all
the noises right and left. He crept close, raised his head slowly
until his eyes were level with the pane and his nose was pressed
to the glass. Then he clutched his own throat to stifle his own
scream, his heart hurting his chest in one giant convulsion. Immediately opposite his own eyes, separated only by the thickness

of a centimeter, was another face also pressed against the glass. A wild, miniature face, distorted by the contact, grubby with tears, hollow-cheeked and luminous pale. The flattened orb was surrounded by a tangled halo of gold, the eyes china blue, the pink mouth opening and closing like a fish, mouthing words. Slightly above the ledge of the window, higher than the head, there were small hands each side of the staring eyes, clawing at the window with bitten nails. The face began to disappear as if drawing back, breath left on the window from the mouthing of words. "Mine," the soundless voice appeared to be saying, "Mine, Mine, Mine," while the fingers clawed and pointed. His jaw hung slack for a minute: he noticed the nails, chewed to the quick like his own, as his eyes remained locked, fixed on the other hands, smearing the pane, helpless. Transfixed only for the moment, the terror then reached his feet: he staggered, stumbled wildly to the extreme end of the garden, not the way he had come in, but crashing over a medium wall and a flimsy trellis on the other side, stumbling forward to another building, down some steps to collide with a basement door, knocking at it and gibbering like an animal while he hit at the window in the top, all caution lost in an agony of terror. The vagrant needed humankind: if they put one arm up his back or stabbed at him or beat him, he still needed them more: could not control his tongue or his own brown and bitten fingers which rapped for attention. He gibbered in his baby language, gibbered more like the child, wanting nothing else than they should let him in.

After the police had come and gone with more indifference than efficiency, carrying away with them this small, filthy adult suffering from dementia, Mrs. Harrison made a cup of tea. Thick and strong with plenty of sugar the way they liked, even more sugar than usual because it was good for shock. Samantha's yelling had added to the distraction and speed of the officers and for this service she was being rewarded with chocolate biscuits. On account of the row, the officials had required minimal information, nor had any of them waited for tea, such a disappointment to one and all in finding nothing more than yet another vagrant in a neighborhood populated with such. "Talks a lot, didn't he?" said Harrison, feeling braver and far more confident in the aftermath. Mrs. Harrison was

simply relieved for the continued absence of the mistress. That old lie about the necklace lay heavy, although what with Mrs. P caring nothing for anything, might not have mattered any longer, but then again, could have been trouble: you never could tell; and besides, second nature dictated she lied at least a little of the time. Keep them in the dark about everything except your own perfections, a habit maintained over years of service for which she never considered herself properly rewarded. Too late to confess now, although, thinking as she did so frequently of Jeanetta, she bitterly regretted the dishonesty imposed on Katherine Allendale, felt profound unease.

"He was just jibbering," she said slowly, "that beggar, talking like a monkey. Must have been frightened by something, I don't know. Kept trying to pull the blighters into the garden, but there wasn't anything there. All that fiddling, pointing with his fingers and waving his hands round his head. Bit touched, poor devil. But he must have seen something, or why knock?"

"He must have wanted catching. Comfortable inside, isn't it? Better than being out in the rain. Must have been the rain that did it. He was talking foreign, I thought, in bits."

"How would you know?" she jeered at him.

"I don't know, but I couldn't make it out, so it can't have been English, can it?"

"Probably saying thank you to you for letting him in. Like you did last time. Here, open the windows, it stinks in here."

Harrison ignored the jibe and sank into the chair which was the oldest, aged entirely by his own behind, took a sip from the tea mug, shuffling. "What's this, then?" His behind was disturbed by an extra crease, uncomfortable, since he was familiar with every nuance of his favorite chair. "Here, look," he said, retrieving the red shawl from under his behind; "he's gone and left this." The red cloak emerged, filthy and crumpled. "What's he think he is?" Harrison chuckled. "Batman?" Mrs. Harrison grabbed the garment.

"Put it down, you daft man sitting on it, you don't know where it's been." She held the cloak aloft with suspicion, tempered with puzzlement and a frisson of familiarity. "Might have been a nice thing once," she remarked moving toward the fire with the thing held between two fingers. Then she appeared to think again and

shoved it in the bin which contained the rubbish. A number of stranded memories were struggling for connection: she began to take the cloak out of the bin again when the upstairs door banged so loudly the house shook.

"It's Her," said Harrison, "back from the shops. Got herself the usual supplies, by the sounds of it." There was a thump of shopping hitting floor. "Did you have another go at her, after I did, about next door? You said you would?" He knew she had from the way the face clouded. "Shut up," said Mrs. Harrison, "just shut up a minute. Let me think."

The day was so fresh after rain, and her mind so clear she did not want to think. Katherine had slept a sleep which was free of all dreams and even the alarms which followed waking were not disturbing. Such as finding the clothes in her wardrobe had been pruned of almost everything she had acquired without David's guidance, including the suit she had exchanged in the boutique he most frequently preferred. All that remained in the scaled-down collection were clothes which reflected his preferences, severely classical or tarty. Since he had slept late, hugged her without any demands before rising to see amiable Jeremy, putting her first, she was more than disposed to forgive, did not really consider there was anything to forgive although she vaguely regretted the hiding of a pair of jeans. There was nothing nicer in the whole wide world than knowing that she did not have to get up, could stay, if she wished, in the cocoon of that bed, safe.

Tranquility bloomed through the house with Jeanetta absent from it: Katherine set her mind away from anything which could possibly disturb that precious status quo, let herself be fussed over, an exquisite pleasure. Going down to the kitchen, dressed in a neat skirt and favorite cashmere, she found the tidy crumbs which signified their breakfast, wondered where the men had gone, feeling absurdly cosseted and happy. The basement, perhaps: Jeremy adored the workshop below stairs. Katherine looked inside the fridge, found sliced cold beef, and suppressing the hurt which arrived with the knowledge of how well he had looked after himself the day before, took two slices. She could have her own way today; anything she wanted was hers. Eleven o'clock: a sandwich as good as anything, and she began, with gaiety, to construct one.

THE PLAYROOM

Oh what to do with the day, nothing for preference: exhaustion was still lurking despite the refreshment of such a calm and blissful morning. From the garden end of the kitchen, the radio was playing softly. Surprising for such a self-sufficient man to need so much music, but he said the sound soothed the boy. Her handbag was still on the kitchen floor, nasty little memory of some time ago, the sight occasioning a guilty memory, only subdued by her recovering from inside the apples she had placed there, washing them and returning them to the fruit bowl. So tired still, so very tired. She walked to a mirror on the wall by the windows to the garden, examined her hair: what a mess, a frightful bush full of wisps and sticking-up tufts, must remember never to sleep with damp hair. He would never make her cut it now. Using both hands, she pulled back the mane, looking around for something to tie it, sighing. It was only then, close to the playroom door, she could hear an echoing sigh, absorbed in a sound which seemed to come from a great distance, a kind of singing.

"Rainy, rainy rattlestones. Go away . . . and break his bones . . ." A pause for breath in the tuneless droning, immediately resumed. "Pussycat, pussycat . . . Where you been? He's been up to London to . . . something the Queen. Miaow . . ." the line and the subdued voice trailing away into a cough. The cough was politely subdued, as if not part of the repertoire.

Katherine moved like a marionette legs refusing to bend. She jerked back to the table where her beef sandwich sat on a plate. Jeanetta with Sophie, gone to stay with silly Granny, oh good, he had said, he wouldn't lie, would have left the door to the playroom locked whatever, he always did, all the doors. This was imagination, rain playing tricks, spoiling everything and spoiling her turn to be spoiled. She looked at the sandwich, granary bread, beef and a little mustard to spice the taste in her mouth. Reached in an unlocked drawer for a piece of polythene, wrapped her breakfast and put it in the handbag. Rose from this stooping to the floor and jerked back across the room, not looking at the playroom door, and turned up the volume of the radio.

18

SOPHIE HAD FOUND THE CAT ON SUNDAY MORNING. MARSHALING HER energies, although these seemed to lack direction whatever she did, she had traveled on the threatening tube line and alighted at the wrong stop for the house of her son. Knowledge of the losses in her burglary made her abstemious enough for public transport: otherwise she could not tolerate less than a taxi or walking, which was her preference provided she need go no more than half a mile without a little rest. In the whole of her dependent life, she had never arrived on the doorstep of her son unannounced: the sheer temerity of her expedition made her nervous. Then the lack of consideration showed by a train driver in depositing her so deliberately at the wrong stop, especially after she had waited in surroundings of sublime ugliness for the thing to arrive, angered her to the extent she walked away from the wrong station muttering something along the lines of how she would never darken their doors again. Only two stops wrong, so small a space on that map on the wall of the tunnel. Looked as if you only walked in a straight line, no distance at all. But she came out of the station and lost her bearings, encountered a main road leading to another road twice as busy. Looking for a quieter street, she fell into a small Sunday market where music played from stalls and clothes of all

colors were for sale. This was the cause of half an hour's distraction and a total expenditure of three pounds sterling. Parting with the money in those small, bright coins which always reminded her of chocolate currency consumed at Christmas, she refused to think of how closely the sum approximated to a taxi fare between her own violated house and that of her grandchildren.

Such a notion could hardly count when she had just purchased for them both a pair of luminous socks, also a pair for David. He would scoff, of course: but it would show she had remembered his birthday. The only hope was that the mellowness of that occasion would have leaked into this weekend before the event, enough to make her welcome although she was breaking all the rules. Enough to allow him to admit her unannounced, or make him explain why her last cry for help, in the middle of the night for heaven's sake, had met with so little response. Well, no response. Which would be the problem to face if only she could begin to discover exactly where she was. At the moment she saw the cat, she wanted to sit down and howl; repeating howlings of all their names in order to bring them to her side and scold them for putting her old body to such trouble, and also because she was lost.

She had set out so bravely, muttering all the evening before, "Now listen here, David: what d'you think you're up to, old tricks again, mmm? I'm your mother, just you listen to me . . ." All of this bravado might have faded on his doorstep, but she could not find his doorstep. Somewhere in a mass of flyovers, underpasses, a pedestrian in a jungle of cars, the courage faded sooner. She sat by the side of the road, counting her money and weeping, and the cat came and rubbed against her legs, keening in tune with her own, quiet moaning.

Since the burglary, she had been brave and organized, but occasionally found all her senses slipping, everything changing as she watched some of her instincts undergo a kind of metamorphosis. The nondescript animal at her feet was nothing she would ever have adopted normally. Far too dirty, scarred by a fight, limping, with matted ears and one malfunctioning eye, ugly as sin even taking misadventure into account. Sophie looked at it, remembered she was alive, and who she was. "Go away," she said, "get off, you dreadful thing. Ugh." The ringing tones of her carrying

voice would have graced a military parade ground, but there was no one to appreciate the evidence of command. "Go A-way," she repeated, then looking down at the matted ear, speaking in an even greater confusion of memory, added, "Please, oh do get off, please." The cat arched around her ankles as a lorry thundered by. "You shouldn't be here, really you shouldn't," Sophie went on, rubbing her shins, quite liking the sensation. Then the thing began to move toward the road and she noticed how small it was. Not a cat proper, a kitten, mangled by fortune and even more bereft of street wisdom than herself, scuttling toward the traffic. Perhaps it had thought she was going to kick it, oh my dear, what a thought, as if she would. "Stop," she commanded, "stop at once." The small rump wobbled in response to a draught raised by a passing car. Sophie leapt forward, dropping the socks and her handbag, scuttled back to the safety of the wall with one bundle of fur. She stuffed it in the front of her best jacket and picked up her bag, noticing the dirt on her hands and the lace of her cuffs. She felt the bizarre elevation of having stolen something, and somehow, what with that and the filth, it was not quite possible to carry on to David's house.

"An absolute dice with death, my dear. Really, I didn't know I had it in me. Practically under the wheels of a juggernaut. Isn't that right, pussy? Nice taxi man brought us home."

"For nothing?" Mary asked caustically, doubting with her usual consistency any act which even smelled of philanthropy. So far the saga of all these events had taken longer than planned. She had only intended a passing visit, an interlude in the desert of Sunday afternoon, which was even worse than Saturday. If there had been a point to this story, other than one disgusting animal lying on a hearthrug, she had begun to forget, as the teller intended.

"We paid the man, of course." Sophie was not about to repeat the episode of offering him the luminous socks in lieu. "Anyway, that's why I never got to David's."

"Why were you going?" Mary asked. "Did they ask you? Shouldn't you phone and explain why you never got there? It's three o'clock. You know how they are about Sunday lunch. Or any lunch."

"They didn't ask me, as it happens," Sophie stated after some

hesitation. "I was just going to go. Time that boy was sorted out. Really. Never coming to see me after I was burgled, appalling behavior. Not Katherine either."

"Oh, Sophie, sweetheart, I am sorry. And about your burglary. How absolutely awful. You should have phoned me."

"I didn't want you," said Sophie with devastating dignity. "I wanted Katherine."

Mary was shocked into silence, standing to one side of Sophie's chair with her fists clenched. "Not at first," Sophie continued artlessly, "I wanted David, of course. And the children, more than anything. Something to hug." Her brow wrinkled in the effort of concentration. "I haven't seen my own grandchildren for weeks. But then I wanted Katherine, nice, sweet Katherine. She's always been nice to me. She understands me, you see."

"Katherine didn't come either, though," Mary snapped. "Shows how sweet, how kind, doesn't it?" She had not meant to sound so waspish. Guilt and rejection hardened her.

"I wouldn't really expect her to come over here," said Sophie. "They'll be having a party next week, I expect, for his birthday. They usually do. She'll be busy, and anyway, she should rest, in her condition."

"What condition?"

"Why, another baby of course, David thinks. That's why I had to go today, not really because of the burglary. But then I got lost and then this kitten and then, oh, I don't know, I came home. I'll go tomorrow. They don't answer the phone. Always engaged or always out. Busy, I suppose."

"Which indicates sound health all round." Mary was still sharp, but the beginning of a familiar worry was nagging. She was beset with visions she could not quite understand: Katherine, pale as a ghost in a restaurant, wanting to confess. Katherine in front of the depiction of adultery, blushing and sweating. A Katherine pregnant not quite equating with the same person rolling around with a lover on hot afternoons. Not the Lover she knew, every inch the pragmatic Frenchman, he was, every single inch: careful with passion, but passionately careful. She knew all about him, and also how sick pregnancy was like to make her sister. The worry grew.

"Sound health?" Sophie repeated. "What's that got to do with anything?" She bent to tickle the cat, which was entirely at home.

"Something's wrong in that house. Something terribly wrong."

"Oh, surely not . . . too much luxury . . ."

"Yes, yes," Sophie insisted, not without relish. "I know there is. David may be having a bad patch."

"Rubbish, I'm sure he's fine: they've got plenty of money."

"I don't mean that kind of patch. He has turns, you see. Locks himself up and broods. Oh not violent or anything, not really. The psychiatrist said it was all something to do with anxiety."

"Which psychiatrist?" Mary almost shouted. The thought of psychiatrists made her ill. Sophie turned pale-blue eyes on her. The dislike in them was veiled by a vagueness only half deliberate. "Oh, long, long time ago. When he was a teenager and finally got Daddy sent to prison. Daddy stole all his things, so he locked Daddy up and when Daddy came out he went on the rampage. David didn't hit him first of course, he never hits anyone first. But then," she added with apparent irrelevancy, "Daddy was very untidy. He'd always taken away everything David and I had and David didn't like that. He was a bully, Daddy. I'm glad he's dead." This was said with prim precision.

"A long time ago," Mary echoed, letting Sophie hear the disbelief in her voice. "Nothing to do with the present. Katherine's causing the trouble. I know she is, not David. Katherine always causes trouble. I can't tell you how, but she does."

Sophie turned eyes back to the cat, hiding the impatience, privately wishing to be left alone with the newer and less demanding friend. She should have thought of a cat long ago. "Katherine never meant harm to anyone in her life," she said with finality. "Would you like some tea?" The invitation was not enthusiastic.

"No thank you. I must dash. Will you go again tomorrow?"

"Yes, of course. Unless they phone." She hid from Mary an expression of fear. Of the roads and the train and the confusion, as well as the reception she might have at the other end. Resolution was waning and Mary could not follow the undertones. "Certainly I shall. Or perhaps the day after. I'll have to look after this baby creature, won't I? Why don't you go?"

Well, why not? The rain began as Mary tap-tapped home. Her steps were even and determined. Katherine had once told her she walked with the same-sized steps all the time as if trying to avoid

the cracks in the pavement. Or trouble of the kind created by superstitions, the past and every color of emotion. The steps were systematic but agitated. Maybe she had got everything wrong, but Mary knew she was never mistaken, not ever, and most of what she thought on the subject of her sister's family was still subsumed in anger, licking around colder thought processes like a flame. Silly Sophie wanted Katherine; so. Dear David adored Katherine to distraction, as had, and did, Claud; so. David had a muddy past, so. Weren't they all made for each other, so what. Mary stopped at a corner shop for food, comforting carbohydrate, tea cakes, biscuits, rubbishy company for the last of the afternoon. Thinking and munching butter and sweet things to clear the mind and add to the guilt. There was nowhere on Sunday to take tea: luxury should begin at home. She added to her purchases three bunches of half-dead flowers, the kind reserved for sale on the sabbath to people with more money than sense, but enough to alleviate the white of her unmarked walls. The white reminded her of duty, and all the institutions which had ever spelled security; she wanted to blot it out. She thought of Katherine in hospital, white walls. Another baby, well, well, well. Three for you and none for me: let Sophie help you: I shan't.

It was only later, after that strange phone call, that she thought of the best trick of all. No good keeping quiet and pretending she was not worried: worry about Katherine was an ingrained habit and telling herself she had no responsibility at all to prevent the silly little creature from mucking up her life and not contacting her mother-in-law, was a repetition which palled and was fading fast. There was a compromise in there somewhere, which would fulfill the duty and avoid all contact with a sister she could not bring herself to see. More than one compromise, but first things first. So she telephoned Susan Pearson Thorpe.

Mary's black telephone book was not quite comprehensive enough to contain the numbers of her sister's neighbors, although it did include on the well-thumbed pages, so many of Katherine's friends and every kind of professional contact under the sun, all the charities, plumbers and doctors active in central London. The name of Pearson Thorpe rang a bell, large person, mentioned by Katherine as the next-door neighbor where the children resorted every day, and there could not be so many Pearson Thorpes in the

book. Mary rehearsed her inquiries, "I'm so sorry to bother you on a Sunday evening but I can't raise my sister, would you happen to know if they've gone away?" No, not raise my sister, sounded like something coming up out of a tomb. That thought was suddenly frightening, equally soon dismissed as nonsense, if only she could control the images in her mind instead of thinking like a child, thinking in colors and pictures as Katherine always had, crippled by imagination. There, she had found and dialed the number. She had even got halfway through the spiel in her authoritative voice before she sensed the hostility. Or the fact that the woman on the other end of the line was not quite following anything which was said.

"K'thrine A'dale? Sister, who she? Oh, yes, yes, yes yes. Got you. Whatchyou phoning me for?"

"Being a bit of nuisance, I'm afraid . . ."

"Not a bit of it. Nobody ever calls me. Pity. Whatcha want, again? No, I don't think they're away. Who was it? Oh dear, sorry."

There was a muffled thump, as if someone, or something heavy had fallen to the ground. Mary held the phone away from her ear. There was a very loud clearing of the throat. "Whoopsy daisy," said the voice, slipping into a short giggle, curtailed by a hand across the mouth.

"Perhaps Mr. Pearson Thorpe could help," said Mary in her best voice of endless patience. The smothered giggle turned into a snort.

"You betcha he could. He could help a lot. He's gone off, though."

"Well anybody who might have seen my sister, really. I'm sorry to ask, but their phone doesn't seem to work . . ."

"Ah." There was the heavy breathing of labored thinking. This woman is drunk, Mary thought: God help Katherine with her neighbors and what the hell is going on with the kids. "Tell you what," said the voice, gathering speed and clarity. "You wan' Mrs. Harr-is-on, not me. She always knows allll about nex' door. All about it."

"About what?"

"Nothing. She thinks a lot. I'll get her. Now. Wait a minute. I couldn't give a toss about nex' door. Nor a fart. Wait a minute . . ."

By this means, with patience worn thinner than a thread, Mary

came to speak on a Sunday evening to Mrs. Harrison, total stranger, and they came to reassure one another. It was all very simple. Mrs. Harrison poured forth into the ear of Mary Fox all the worries she had never succeeded in imparting to her employer, who would not listen. The worries had been incubated into a state of incoherence, and the television boomed in the background. She talked long and excitedly about not seeing the eldest child, Katherine's first-born, in as many weeks as the child had years. She gabbled about the little boy, fine, oh yes perfectly fine, out with Daddy. Then she accelerated into children's tales about a thinner version of little Jeanetta sitting in the garden, singing to herself, thereby giving, quite inadvertently, the impression, that this had been yesterday. Then there was news of a party the Allendales were having on Tuesday or was it Wednesday, all information spewed forth in a rush and an irritating accent. Mrs. Pearson Thorpe would see everyone then, said Mrs. Harrison. She would be able to check. Mary doubted Mrs. Thorpe's powers of observation in any context, and was aware that she had not been invited to any party. Lastly, there was something incomprehensible about a man coming to the door with a cloak which this Mrs. Harrison had seen before.

"Jeanetta loved to dress up," she explained.

"Just like her mama," Mary added into a split-second silence.

She was beginning to think the whole household was mad, regretting the phone call in earnest. Nothing she had heard was raising alarm bells too loud to ignore, but the woman would not stop, even when Mary started to pity her sister for living adjacent to a pair of harridans. The very word came to mind, and with it something which was expedient as well as a practical joke. She remembered Sophie's dreadful new pet, was reminded of cats and charity workers, oh what a joke. In another frame of mind, less sharpened by rejection and less irritated, Mary would never have thought of what she considered now. She would never willfully waste anyone's time.

"Listen, Mrs. Harrison, I'll tell you what I'll do. You say you've been round and they don't let you take the child out, never mind. But if you're seriously worried about the children, have you considered phoning the authorities?"

"Oh, no, I couldn't do that, really I couldn't. What would people say? I just couldn't."

"Well, I could. Better than any of us, wouldn't it? Someone to check? Then we'd certainly know if there was anything up. I know just the chap to ask."

"Oh no, it's not that bad . . ." Mrs. Harrison was backtracking, embarrassment oozing from every pore. ". . . I'm sure everything's all right really. I've tried to get Mrs. Pearson Thorpe to go but . . ."

"I quite understand," said Mary smoothly. "Well, we'll send the chap, shall we? Then we'll know for certain sure and you won't need to worry ever again."

"Yes," said Mrs. Harrison, after a long pause to weigh up all the pros and cons. "Yes, that would be for the best. Oh, thank you."

"Tomorrow," said Mary. "Today's Sunday."

"I know," said Mrs. Harrison. "I don't like it, but I'll sleep easy now."

"Goodnight, then," said Mary. The official, reassuring voice was all Mrs. Harrison heard.

The reassuring voice gave itself a little more to eat, marveling that food was such a good, if temporary panacea. Laughing to itself for such a coup of an idea. Good old Child Action Volunteers, the perfect people, with John Mills the very perfect sort of pest to inflict on that perfect household. He would lean on a nest of tables and splinter the wood: he would mar the perfection: he would offend Katherine with his shambling presence and he would infuriate David with his persistence. And Mary would have done her duty, just in case there was anything really wrong. He was certainly best for the task; if there was anything wrong, he would find it. Had a reputation after all, as well as perfect, utterly reliable reports. A sweet combination for maximum effectiveness, and a very large element of revenge. Tomorrow would do. Sunday was a day of rest. It wasn't as if, on the basis of all these flapping old women, there was any panic at all. Like Mrs. Harrison, Mary slept easy.

John Mills had almost forgotten what it was like to sleep by the time he recognized the presence of Monday morning. When he had returned home from a mild day's work on the Saturday evening, to find his flat bereft of animal life, he had panicked before

he went back out to look for them, pacing the streets, stopping people and asking questions. Many of those interrogated en route for Saturday-night pleasures resented the interruption while bowing to his insistence since he was clever at making an "excuse me" feel like a blow. "Excuse me, but have you seen a stray cat? Or one, or two, or three?" his face illuminated with urgency and the twitch below the eye working overtime. Responses varied between, Yes, seventeen cats, Don't think so, Pardon? and No, I fucking haven't, piss off. The irritation would have been less if he had not always repeated his question, were they quite sure they had not seen stray cats, I mean, absolutely sure. He asked similar questions in shops and pubs like a man repeating a litany of prayers and in between said little else but oh dear, oh dear, or made strange noises toward the alleys between houses and even toward drains. With rare logic, he did not take his questions to the takeaway downstairs from the flat. They were busy and besides friendly enough to have returned his properties had they found them. "I don't understand," he kept repeating on his return; "I just don't understand. Why would anyone come in just for kittens? No stereo this time, no telly, just cats, I can't work it out." Matilda had been silent and restless, jumping each time he spoke although he did not notice. "Other people might love them as much as you," was the last she had snapped, turning away. Because of his tossing, turning and mumbling, or so he presumed, she went to sleep on the sofa reserved for their rare guests, and early in the following morning, went out. For the day, her note stated, not unkindly. Will be back. In the normal event, such a missive would have distressed him. As it was, he did not care for company.

The thought gradually occurred that no one deliberate enough to steal a crate of kittens would be likely to leave them around in the locality for the owners to find at leisure. Whatever had been the purpose of so odd and tidy a piece of burglary, via roof or door, he knew not, he hoped the motives were benign. Visits to terrible estates had once forced him to witness cats being stoned: cats being coated with paraffin and . . . But by evening, he had persuaded such images out of his mind and made himself imagine the whole furry collection assembled elsewhere, in front of a fire, perhaps, a better home than this. Matilda's silence on any subject

was a matter of indifference. On Sunday, he slept better, still fitful; waking at dawn to curse himself for his failures and his own stupidity.

For God's sake, going round the houses and never looking at his own. The nether regions other than the roof formed areas he had never explored, go to it. At this bright suggestion, Matilda shot out of the flat two hours early for work, muttering something about errands, and he went downstairs. He was still heavy with grief, not optimistic for anything at all when he found the back door to the yard, not locked, resigned himself to nothing, whistling as he went out in pursuit of one, last chance. Oh, dear God, what God, there never was a God. Only a devil with an army.

Such a pathetic amount of blood in that confined space among the weeds, plenty enough to indicate death as well as agony. Scratched on to the remains of two cardboard boxes moist from the rain which had fallen overnight, gore in spots dark against the broken concrete of the ground. In one corner, Kat, her long body described in one ugly arc defined by her dead fur, each limb reduced to bone by the wet. The legs were stretched, the teeth bared and her back broken in a sharp angle. By the bowl still full of water for an absent dog, John found one of the kittens, neck snapped and distended, the little abdomen punctured in one massive wound, and against one wall, amid drifting balls of fur, another corpse, curled peacefully but without the fluffy tail he had often stroked. Half of a head; so little blood. He closed his eyes against the screaming, yowling, shrieking episode, the tornado of sight and sound which had made this carnage, heard and saw it all the same, driving his face against a cold brick wall to graze his skin. He moved slowly, edged dead Kat gently with the toe of his shoe before lifting her off the ground, imagined as he did so the sound of cracking bones. Then he was sick into the bowl belonging to the dog, and stood there, holding the wet bundle of fur, not crying, but howling like a beast, the blood on his own face not yet congealed.

"Sorry, very sorry: he's out at the moment . . ." Oh shit where is he? When the indispensable man arrived for work, he was a whole hour later than expected. His steps up the stairs were audible, the same pace as an old man. When he opened the door

and showed them his scratched face, gray but washed, no one noticed the difference and the phone began to ring.

There was something Mrs. Harrison loved about Mondays, any Mondays, but especially this Monday. Madam upstairs went to work for a start, didn't she, so the world started going round again as per normal, thank you. The air was fresh, these silly rainfalls the signal for autumn and the winter she preferred with all those snug evenings with the TV and no need to pretend to be busy because the light was still there. And yes, Mr. Pearson Thorpe was bringing Mark home today and no need to worry about anything else, not perfect, this status quo, but perfectly workable. She sat on the step with her cigarette and surveyed the street. Nice, until him next door came out with all the reminders of other anxieties and daft things said. Looking carefully, but keeping her pose studiedly casual, Mrs. Harrison watched David Allendale coming down the steps, carrying Jeremy like the Crown Jewels in one arm, a pushchair in the other. Because she found it so difficult to forgive him for his response to her own visits to the same front door from which he emerged, Mrs. Harrison did not emit any large hallos, or expect him to either talk or notice her presence, simply looked the other way while watching out of the corner of her eye. That boy was too big for a pushchair, make him walk, toughen him up a bit, could see Dad's point if they were going to a supermarket, all walking kids a bloody liability. Where were they going, never mind, probably shops, nowhere else on Monday. They trundled away uphill, the child chirping like a sparrow, pointing and twisting in his father's arms, Oh for Christ's sake look at them, why had she ever worried about the whole damned family. Your eyes, said husband Harrison, are bigger than your brain.

In the confidence of Monday morning, another idea occurred amid the sunshine and the everything all right with the world sensations. Mrs. Harrison suffered one last stab of guilt which spurred her into action. She checked that the key to the house was in her pocket, clambered down the steps, minced up the street while throwing away the fag and went up the steps to the Allendales, all of this done with a bit of puff and a rhyme itching inside her head from Samantha's repetition of this morning. Bugger rhymes: sometimes she wished she knew fewer, but could never

resist the singing. Nothing else to say, Harrison said: you never got out of the nursery. How did it go, easy.

> Miss Polly had a dolly which was sick, sick, sick,
> She sent for the doctor to come quick, quick, quick;
> The doctor came with his bag and his hat
> And knocked on the door with a rat-a-tat-tat.

"Tick, tick, tick," said Samantha.

No, no, Mrs. Harrison had scolded, wrong bits of words, thinking like this while she knocked at the door with a rat-a-tat-a-tat, ignoring the brilliant polish of the bell. She waited for a response, wishing she had not thrown away the cigarette half done, slightly nervous in case the master should return all of a sudden and find her there. There was a lengthy delay before the door was opened, slowly and far from wide like you would if you intended a welcome. In the small space through which Mrs. Harrison peered, her own face obscured by the sun behind her but nevertheless transfixed in an artificial grin, Mrs. Harrison saw Katherine. Even at 10:00 A.M. in her own home, hair brushed, pressed camel slacks in cool gabardine, a white blouse and a tiny row of pearls soothing the neck. None of these accoutrements prevented Mrs. Harrison from noticing that the other was extremely pale and apparently thinner than ever, but then again, clothes were terribly deceptive. Nothing worth any kind of remark.

"Hallo, Mrs. Allendale. Lovely morning. How are you? Listen, I was just wondering: I was going to be taking Samantha up the park, you know, to the swings . . . Shall we take Jeanetta too? Might give you a break if you want. Lovely day," she repeated.

Katherine opened the door a trifle wider, looked anxiously up the street in the direction her husband had taken, took a step back. She seemed to struggle for composure, put her hand over her mouth and coughed painfully, then straightened her narrow spine and smiled.

"Excuse me, got a cough."

"Oh dear," clucked Mrs. Harrison automatically, "Nasty."

"Both of us, actually," Katherine continued. "Jenny and me. Flu or something, but she can't come to the park, Mrs. Harrison.

She's gone off, you see, to stay with her granny. You've met Granny, I'm sure."

"Can't say I did," Mrs. Harrison replied.

"Oh, I thought you must have done." Katherine thrust a strand of hair behind one ear. "She lives out of town, in the country. Jeanetta loves it there, she gets so spoiled, she won't want to come back. They eat nothing but biscuits." Both of them stood there smiling at one another.

"Well, that's all right then," said Mrs. Harrison. "Very nice for them, I'm sure."

"Yes," said Katherine. "It is, actually. I miss her."

"Well, yes. I expect you do. Nice, though, the peace and all that."

"Yes, very nice. Ever so nice."

There were a few other words about days being lovely before Mrs. Harrison, still missing the cigarette, scurried home. Oh dear, oh dear, how silly she had been, her tongue sticking to the roof of her mouth in one great scolding of herself; I don't know, I really don't.

Embarrassing, all of it, really. " 'S all right," she yelled to Harrison as she came indoors, "everything all right," as if he had even asked to know. No response, which made her crosser. Everything all right and every bugger should need to know. What a fool. She wished she had found the sense to take the number of that sister woman, whose voice had been so bossy, that one, last night, how stupid not to take down something like they always did on the TV, in offices. Then she could have called her back before the woman phoned her tomorrow like she promised, told her not to bother with whatever it was she was about to bother with. No one should worry at all, nor should they. All that stuff we watch, she said to Harrison, makes us think too much; we imagine things. What things? Things which bump in the night.

The front door closed behind him. Katherine did not ask where he had been, what constitutional he had taken with Jeremy by his side like a guardian angel, the one to the other. When he arrived in the kitchen, she was standing at the business end with her hands in the kitchen sink, and as he breezed into the room with arms full of food shopping, he did not cease to smile when he saw the

direction of her gaze. Placed his packages on the table and came across to her side for one, brief hug. She did not respond.

"Mrs. Harrison came," she said dully. "I told her you-know-who had gone to stay with her granny. Like you told me." Without comment, both had ceased to mention the name which had dropped entirely from any conversation.

"That's right," he said cheerfully. "So she has. Having a great time."

"But it isn't right. You know exactly where she is. Here. You lied, David." She pointed with one trembling arm in the direction of the silent playroom door. He placed his hands on her shoulders.

"Katherine, my sweet, be sensible. Why don't you change your clothes and go out for a while, hey? The gym? Shopping? Nothing too strong, darling: You're not so well. Plenty pocket money, big treat. Lovely outfit for you to collect. For tomorrow night. My birthday present to you."

Katherine stared, the eyes in the middle distance, a puzzlement crease developing over her forehead.

"But she isn't staying with Granny. She's there, you-know-who, behind that door. Not with Sophie. We should get her out. Why doesn't Sophie ever phone anymore? She never phones like she used to phone, does she, David?"

His voice sank to a level she could perceive as dangerous. His hands were full of warning.

"Katherine, listen. There'd be so much trouble if you let her out. Prison and everything, I promise you. No one would recognize her. You'd be locked up, like I told you, how many times?" Katherine shrank back, hugging her arms to her chest and whispered.

"Did you look today?"

There was very slight hesitation. "Yes. No, of course not. Why would I do that? How silly you are. It's very simple. You know very well she's gone to stay with Sophie. Granny. Repeat that after me. Then go out and say it again, only louder. Go on, say it now. So I can hear you."

"She's gone to stay with her granny. She's gone to stay with her granny. She's gone to stay with her granny."

"Good, good girl. Very good girl. Now don't forget collecting that dress. I'm going to start with the stuff for tomorrow evening. You could always buy me something for my birthday. I shall make

myself a cake, with candles." He beamed on her, his face containing all the innocent pleasure of a schoolboy while her face was held in the spotlight of his smile.

"Will you give her some?" The smile faded.

"I can't, Katherine, you know I can't. Say it again, what I told you."

She tussled with memory and then her brow cleared. She raised her hands as if to conduct an orchestra, waved them level with her shoulders in the effort to repeat, carefully controlling the words.

"I know, I know, I know. Now I know. She's gone to stay with Granny."

"That's right," he said. "Absolutely right. Now we all know. You're a good baby and I love you to pieces. Who's a good little girl then?"

"I am. She's gone to stay with Granny."

He tapped the underneath of her chin lightly and playfully. "Very good girl. Look, I've bought us sweeties . . ."

19

GLORY, GLORY, ALLELUIA. NOTHING EVER STAYS THE SAME. BECAUSE I thought this was not the case, I thought there was nowhere else to go but down and anyway, looking up hurt the head more than somewhat. I'm so sorry, though, about that poor woman with the officious voice who phoned last night: Oh, dear, I have always been rude, abrupt and indifferent, but slopping drink and words down the phone in equal proportions excelled most other efforts in that line. Not a matter for self-congratulation. Nothing about me worthy of praise: *in vino veritas*, a slug, a worm, a nasty piece of goods. I was stoking up and well lit up, preparing for another onslaught on another week, another bit of my life which looked set to slip away and I wanted Sebastian so much the whole of me screamed. The thought of his returning on the Monday evening, saying his goodbyes, agreeing perhaps, for the sake of form and my fallen face, to come to the neighbors' party with me, was all too much. So I practically took the gin through a straw. Then I fell over. When I woke up, I wanted to die.

Monday morning, dawn, was thus the very end of the world. There was rain in the air, better than all the heat which created the wet, but dark rain, an unspoken storm making the sky bleak

and I could not believe it was seven in the morning and cold as ice. There is a tautness to the face which comes from drink. In a way, it flatters my looks, smooths out the skin suffused from all that fluid, the same plumping out of a baby in tears, soft, flushed skin and the true state of health only showing in the pink whites of the eyes, as if one had swum in chlorine for half the night. All I had to do was reconstruct the visage with all those expensive cosmetics bought in one optimistic day, stagger to work via the well-known route, blind as a bat. Despite the investment of my life in the whole business of work, My career, My office, My everything, bolstered by the loyalty of clients as abrasive as me, I am well aware that my sacking is on the agenda. I should have been aware far sooner than this, having sacked others for lesser crimes than indifference and pink, babyish, early morning faces. I have sacked them for devotion to their families, God help me: work and selfishness came first, emotional impoverishment or the quality of life not my concern. It is now. We old soaks, you see, need to have an element of insight forced upon us and we resist to the last ditch. I do not think I have noticed a single thing about the life of anyone around me for months, possibly years, but, as I said, God is good when he is not a bastard: things change.

Sitting in the office, doing nothing but nursing the head, I could hear noises off, like a whispering behind scenes in a play which is going wrong. Regular whispering: just like home: Mrs. Harrison, Mr. Harrison, Samantha, Mark, chuntering behind the door, saying, "Shall we go in?" Sebastian, too, saying out of earshot, shall I go home: will she talk to me this evening, no, better to stay: there will be no food, no comfort, no nothing at home, and could I ever make love to her any other time but early morning when she does not even notice . . . ? I am so used to whispers behind my back, whisperings reminiscent of some hated head prefect at school, talked about from a good distance in case the bully should hear. I should have listened to the whispers, not merely shouted back, but I've started now. Perhaps I can learn a little sensitivity after all.

Mark did it, seven-year-old Mark, that child of charm brought up mainly by others. They went off to the sea, my husband, whom everybody loves and I had ceased to notice, and Mark, joyous son, to look at waves and do manly things like play pinball machines

in arcades and have fun. Consume fish and chips like starving creatures and make entertainments together, I don't know what, I didn't ask. But Mark fell over some spike in the sand, and cut open the soft calf of his leg, first thing Monday morning, I gather. That was what the whisperings in the office were about, should we tell her he phoned before she got in here? With a garbled story about a little boy, oh so small (all those little things in a suitcase), hurt badly, Mrs. Pearson Thorpe, don't know how bad. Your husband phoned from hospital. They think they'll be coming home in the afternoon. Don't worry.

Worry? Not for a minute. All these defenses going into overdrive, me being brisk and saying, Well what about that, silly little sod, what'd he do that for, and where did you say they were? Don't rightly know, to be precise, they said: somewhere on some coast, coming back later. How badly hurt? Don't know either: can't be so bad or they'd keep him in hospital, wouldn't they? But he's broke his leg, as well as cut it, your husband said don't fret, kids is strong and doctors know what to do. Knowing as I do the level of sheer incompetence in all worlds including my own, I doubted all the time who would know what, but I never doubted Sebastian acting for the best. Apart from being such an incompetent ass, such a fool, to let this happen in the first place, I at least understood complete relief about the company my son kept while hurting himself. Sebastian is built to ensure survival. I made my excuses, went home, making myself slow down.

I was only going home to wait, it was better not to hurry. Coming down the street as I was coming up, I ran into Katherine Allendale. Running was not quite the word, since I was running, she, I seem to recall, jerking from one paving stone to the next, carrying a carrier bag, don't know why I could bear to stop. Memories of her sister on the phone the night before, whatever that was about, memories of a number of things, including my lost qualities of politeness, made me hesitate enough to speak. How's things, Katherine? I remembered children, I thought of nothing but children, and how were hers, not wanting to know, but for once, wanting to ask. She said it three times if she said it once; everything fine, do you know, Jeanetta has gone to stay with her granny. Yes, I heard you, I said, how nice for them both. Yes it is, actually, she answered. And where are you going? Me, driven by the same

politeness, trying to postpone the news from home. I'm going to the gym, she said. I looked at her, forgetting she was a thief, my rival, my glamorous and pathetic neighbor with the husband I once fancied and the house Sebastian coveted and it crossed my mind she might be a bit mad. Taking that insect figure to that dreadful gymnasium for further refinement. See you tomorrow, she said. What, I said. David's birthday, she said. Dinner. I did not say, Oh no; I simply wanted to say it.

Everything changes. We had all enjoyed health, my family, never thought of health as something one actually enjoyed, simply a condition of life which nothing ever seemed to affect, along with money, property and all that, an automatic assumption of continuance. Our children, like my parents' children, never suffered any accident bar scratches and all this had kept me in a state of innocence, helped me to take it all for granted. So when I sat in the study, waiting the return of the wounded, I admired the insouciance of my soldier father, wished I had seen blood and been able to say, rubbish, only a cut and a boy's a boy. I phoned every hospital on the east coast roughly in the area where I knew they had gone before I drew blanks on five and stopped. No one had said where they were, or I had not listened. I remembered how no one ever tells me the truth. Perhaps they had been trying to avoid telling me the boy was dead.

"Dead: I do hope he isn't dead," such a politely expressed thought crashing into the light like a train out of a tunnel, huge and incapable of being shoved back. So all of a sudden I was winded, had to sit down, fighting back nausea even though I couldn't sit, made little running forays into all corners of the room, a headless chicken skittering backward. Not the ague of drink but the blow to the solar plexus, that sudden vision of his never again being there, nothing more terrible to contemplate than his absence and I cannot begin to describe the horror of this. I may have learned words for feelings while learning a whole new range of the feelings themselves in the few weeks before this, but never enough words to describe these sensations. No Mark: never to see him again, hear him, no child in that seat, no small man espied forever in the corner of my eye, no backdrop to existence. But you scarcely saw him, I told myself: you gave birth crossly and put him to bed, but it does not follow that mothers as indifferent as I could fail to panic

at the prospect of such loss. Late realization of love, call it what you will, but how any woman, even a monster, suffers such a death and survives I do not know. I thought of TV news, children lost in fires or kidnapped, all of this stuff dismissed by me as parental carelessness, and I wanted to weep.

To forestall weeping, I called Mrs. Harrison, gabbled the news. Gabble was right, a turkey rather than a chicken. "Hush," she said, "hush now, don't fret. Nothing to worry . . ." calmer than I but still unable to finish words and twisting her hands in an effort to keep them still. I want to scream, I told her: I just want to scream. Why doesn't Sebastian phone? "I know, I know," she murmured, then brightened. "I know why he doesn't phone," she said. "It's 'cause they're driving home."

This vision worked, I don't know why, simply the thought that you can't drive and telephone at the same time without one of those bloody machines in the car. "They went all the way to Norfolk," Mrs. Harrison said. "I remember, it's a long way, Norfolk. I went there once when I was younger." She laughed nervously at the memory of the distance and probably something else. "Oh, yes, a very long drive." Then she consoled herself cunningly with action, squared her jaw and offered me the same panacea, clever by instinct.

"Listen, Mrs. Pearson, there's things to do. Being as they are on their way home . . ." she stressed the certainty of this, ". . . I've got to do the rooms. Harrison left it all to the last minute, didn't he? All spick and span, we want to be, don't we now?" Her nose wrinkled in distaste as her eyes traveled around my study. "I left Mark's as was, better clear it since he's not so well" (another, clever dismissal of the seriousness). ". . . But you could do in here, if you liked." The old diffidence returning, ". . . Oh, and you could keep Samantha with you, leaves my hands free." In quiet acceptance of her hands being more effective and therefore more important, I took my orders, obeyed without question.

Therapy in action, mustn't fall down, must we, things to do, wise old bird. Giving me chubby Samantha as my companion, so adult, she, so forgiving. How absolutely perverse it was that I should be cleaning and dusting with the clumsiness of no real practice, Samantha equally inept, obeying instructions to be good and telling me jokes, both of us actually enjoying ourselves. It was

bizarre to have such a completely happy couple of hours, anxious but completely absorbed.

"Mummee . . . Here's a good one . . . Why can't you play cards in the jungle?"

"Don't know, darling. You tell me." I was packing surplus paper into a polythene sack.

"Too many cheetahs!" She rolled around on the floor, clutching her sides and laughing like a chimpanzee, though I'm quite sure she has no idea what a real cheater is. "Another?" she said, gasping. "Okay, go on, do."

"What's a crocodile's favorite game?"

"I don't know."

"Go on, guess."

"I can't, that's far too hard for me."

"Snap!" She would shout, jumping on the sofa and kicking her legs in the air, while I laughed too, both of us like that, we love jokes, only I never realized. "Come on," I said, "this is work. Carry this stuff downstairs." "Why, what is it?" She peered inside a sack replete with bottles, old letters and dead flies, some of the bottles not quite empty. "Rubbish," I stated firmly. "I like rubbish," said my daughter.

Still bleak outside, you could forget it was summer, a preternaturally dark day, autumn striding rather than creeping into central London like a colossus and the trees shaking their heads in wild disapproval. Sammy and I crashing sacks down the steps to place by the railings the detritus of two rooms, Mark's and mine, and Sammy insisting on adding hers, but abandoning all labor to run up the street on her stubby legs in order to examine the far more interesting rubbish of everyone else. Monday is rubbish day in this stretch of London, but like many a Monday, they had forgotten to collect. On this day in every seven, the street takes on a polythene life with sacks and bins and God knows what appearing from all over the place, oh what work you could do investigating the lives if you looked inside. Be you never so rich, you still have to take out your trash, only I had never done it before. I kept mine indoors, in my mind.

"Look, look, look . . ." Samantha was ten steps away up the pavement, examining a bag outside the Allendales'. "Mummy, look," a strangled stage whisper louder than a prompt.

"Darling, you shouldn't look at other people's rubbish, not nice, come away."

"Look," she insisted, standing ground, she of the iron will and bossy tendencies so refined in her mama. So I ambled up with studied innocence in my walk, and looked: anything to continue this conspiracy with my suddenly gorgeous daughter. "Doggy must have bit the bag," she said importantly. How observant she is, picking the one bag with a large split.

And I could see why she was interested. No moldy old foodstuffs here. A gray plastic sack (the Allendales would, wouldn't they?—designer rubbish, not put inside ordinary black), split open down one side. Flanked by other gray bags, up-market rubbish, I bet, fish-bones and empty caviar jars, my own bitchy guess, but in the torn bag, colors dripping on the ground, nothing but clothes. My eye was caught and held like a bur on a yellow thing with pink spots, diminutive garment sandwiched in between other smaller garments and a pair of striped pajamas. I should have stopped Sammy, but she pulled at the things, bringing more of them on to the pavement. "This is a nice one, Mummy; why is they throwing it away?" Only the colors danced in her eyes, but I saw more. A swathe, there was, of Jeanetta's clothing, little favorites I recognized out of the new clothes Katherine had bought for Jeanetta that one time weeks before, and stranger still, in the same heap, I thought I saw the dustier, more sophisticated pink of a summer suit I had seen that mother wear when we met not long ago. A new suit, I thought, as well as those striped pajamas, either a replica of the same or a pair of Mark's: I had never checked to see if they had all been returned. "Don't," I repeated to Sammy, "Don't. Put them all back, they'll see us."

"Who will?"

"They will."

She was fascinated like a dog determined to pursue a smell, while I felt the strangest sensation in my bones, so strange, a paralysis worse even than that fear for Mark, a sweeping chill which rooted me to the spot, powerless to stop her while goose-pimples raised on the back of my neck and my mind struggled for thoughts. I was shaking with cold but my arms were rigid with shock: then the light went out: I heard the trees again, and Samantha, screaming in whoops of excitement, howling with joy.

And slipping into the curb with noiseless efficiency, Sebastian's Mercedes with a small, white face peering out from the rear window. White and triumphant, trying to look solemn but really smiling like the hero coming home, my son, never more alive.

Sometimes since, I have wondered, without being at all wistful about it, what it is like to be a child. The son and heir was indeed injured: he had fifteen stitches in one calf and a broken ankle, must have hurt like hell, but all he could see by the time the stitches were inserted, was all the compensations which his little mind understood as bound to follow. Such as, "I won't have to go back to school quite at the beginning of term, will I?" or "Do you think people will want to sign this?" pointing to the modest amount of plaster which decorated his skinny shank. That plaster, such pride: he produced it from the car like a film starlet might produce one high-heeled leg, slowly and with great aplomb, waiting for the whistles and the applause, even enjoying the fact that Samantha, initially so full of welcome and gabbled news, was rapidly filled with jealousy.

"Mummy, will I be able to have some crutches?" Sweet, dozy questions from Mark's bed, where I simply sat and watched him.

"Anything you want," I said. And I meant what I spoke. Anything he wanted, anything within my power either of them wanted. Watching him, without thinking too much, I knew I had hit the bottom only to rise a little. There was nothing more important, nothing to begin to put into the same scale, as this boy, this precious life. Oh, I did not weep: I was even bustling but I knew it well. I love my children. Oh Christ I love them all.

Equally well I knew how sensitive was my husband, delivering back the son and heir and letting me take over, even knowing how clumsy I was. Of course he could have bedded the child, washed him with greater efficiency and skill, done all those things better and quicker than I, but they stood back, the Harrisons and Sebastian. He soothed Sammy with attention, left me to direct the comfort of the patient, guided by his instructions. "No, Mummy, mustn't get it wet, this plaster stuff. Can I have a biscuit? No, a chocolate biscuit, please. And some apple juice? Can I get Adam" (a friend from school, another stranger to me) "to come round and see my leg tomorrow?" Yes, yes, yes, until he was drowsy, some drug in him other than trauma making him slip away al-

though he was fighting to stay awake, muttering as his eyes closed, desperate to inform and receive anything he might have missed in his small world, his questions following no sequence.

"Did the beggar come back?" he asked suddenly from the depths of the pillow.

"Which beggar? A man in a book?"

"You know, the dirty man who got in here and got upstairs when Harrison was watching the cricket. Sammy said he came back." Sammy and Mark had conversed in whispers through the door of the loo, before she was shooed away. ". . . And the police came, Sammy said. I think the beggar took Jeanetta, that's what I think, and that's what Sammy says. Is that why the police came? I missed it . . . ow, that hurts. Jeanetta could have come and seen my plaster . . ."

"What man, darling?"

"That one, you know, you must know. But I wasn't supposed to tell you until Mrs. Harry told you. Or they would take us away, other beggarmen, we'd be kidnapped, she said," he added with sleepy relish.

"Of course you wouldn't. You are a silly-billy."

"But Sammy says they took Jeanetta. Jeanetta isn't there anymore. She was so thin, Mummy."

"Jeanetta's coming back, darling. She's only gone to stay with her granny. I expect she'll be back very soon. She'll be able to write on your plaster." Why the hell was he thinking such irrelevant things? Sickness makes for nonsense: I couldn't remember him mentioning next door's lot for weeks. But then, I had not been paying attention: for all I knew, they may have been discussed ad nauseam. Sitting there in the quiet comfort of his newly tidied room, I got back an almost imperceptible hint of that peculiar coldness I had felt in the street. Mark's beautiful dark eyes were gradually closing and his face was rosily pink. The dog snored in the corner, another indulgence for the patient.

"No, she won't come back. Netta. Anyway, she won't write on my plaster, 'cause she can't write . . ."

"Can't write, night-night. Nice dreams."

"It was ever such a big spike, Mummy . . ."

On my soft way downstairs, treading quietly although there was no need, dizzy with relief and the mind still in overdrive, I won-

dered about this beggar, but there were too many other things of greater importance, just then. Besides, he was a secret, whoever he was, and in my new humility, I was prepared to let them have their secrets, as many as they liked, Mrs. Harrison and all: I could not afford jealousy. The house was warm: the tranquility too precious to disturb. Tomorrow would do. Tomorrow would do for everything except whatever was going to happen next.

The face my husband turned to me was lined with incredible weariness, and in it, I saw all the reflected features of our son. Sebastian had not sat in that chair for so long, the mere sight of him, slightly disheveled, open-necked shirt, all of him creased from the head to the shoes, reminded me suddenly of the man on the park bench. Lonely. Like me, I suppose, making my first admission. I did not feel tension since there was no emotion left: I did not feel awkward because I was more grateful to see him there, and if there ever had been another woman for him to run to (which I knew very well there was not: he never tells lies), I had lost all power for indignation.

"Would you like a drink?" My request, noticing he had made no move to find his own.

"Please." I disinterred the whiskey, the hated whiskey which I loathe, quite proud to present it still full. Then I poured a very small gin, put it ever so slightly beyond the reach of my own hand. That way, I would have to reach every time I wished to sip. I cannot reform all at once; I cannot pretend that I would, any more than I can pretend about anything. Dishonesty, like the jealousy, is not a commodity I could afford.

"Are you going to work tomorrow?" A casually loaded question from him.

"No. I thought I'd take a few days off and amuse the boy. Are you?"

"No."

One sip of the gin, this part required some courage. He was opening his mouth to say something which I interrupted with my words first. I could not let him ask first.

"Will you stay here then? Please."

"Yes."

We did not touch. You do not rush across a room and embrace the spouse who has left you, even if you left him first, or you do

not if you are me. I saw the father of my children, not a newfound lover with nothing at all to reconcile. But I touched his shoulder as I passed to the kitchen, briskly, a very passing gesture which he might have thought was a mistake if he had cared to notice, which I thought he might. It cost me, that little touching, but I did touch first. Then I made some supper for us both, like wives are supposed to do, once in a while. Mrs. Harrison might be proud of me.

20

"DON'T SNAP AT US, JOHN. WE'RE ALL BUSY AND YOU AREN'T THE only one with a head, for God's sake. You moody bastard," fondly said. "What's the matter with you today? You drank too much, or something?"

"Nope. I . . ." Somehow he could never finish the sentences, tore his eyes from the blank sky of the windows and smiled. The lethargy was becoming overpowering. ". . . Only all . . . day, I haven't been able to fathom this bloody message. Why didn't she phone again?"

"It's that woman. A mogul. They don't repeat themselves. But she is a relative and did say it was urgent. I didn't ask why she couldn't intervene, not wise to ask, you told me so. Accept what they say at face value and act on it, no other way; hope they're wrong. You jus' gotta go."

He shuffled, awkward. "Not enough," he muttered, "not enough to justify . . ." fumbled again, ". . . I mean, no screams, no yells, bruises. Simply innuendoes. Parents barring relatives from house, maybe all relatives a pain in the neck, often are. Mother neurotic, often is. Twentieth-century disease . . . enlarged groins, enlarged consciences . . . to say nothing of the expectations . . . what's different?"

"Nothing. As much as we usually get. Sort of message starts, nothing wrong and what there is I'm sure as hell not going to tell you. They're all ambiguous, you know they are. Nobody says what they mean, quite; they put out signals, little screams for help, and that's our strength, recognizing the code. What's the matter? . . . Just because you didn't get that bloody award. Well, we didn't either. I thought you were bigger than that. Okay. I'll send someone else." John stirred, outraged.

"Don't be stupid. Of course I'll go. Have you seen the address?"

"What's that got to do with it? I don't suppose you could possibly give us some sort of report by tomorrow?" she added, knowing she was pushing her luck. "That woman, you know. The complainant. Think of the funding."

He wandered up the street, his favorite and yet most unfavorite street, later on the Monday evening. Or at least the hour felt late, technically well into daylight, but dark with the rainy cloud, full of threats; the sky was distended, releasing nothing, and the sun was dead. John felt little but a dull hatred pulsing against his temples as he plodded along one side of the perfectly maintained pavement, the sweeties in his pocket scratching against his thigh through the thin fabric of cotton, his right hand missing the usual plastic carrier of tins. Nothing in this street which was not subdued to man's most prodigal taste: nothing strictly utilitarian at all. Proceeding in a westerly direction, looking left and right with his arms now linked behind his back like a policeman on patrol, he noted the cars. Mercedes, BMW, tiny new Renault, small enough for the wife's runabout or a toy for the servant. Bastards. John knew this street so exactly from his daily passage, he was always surprised to notice more, disgusted himself by the ignorance which never read numbers and had never given him to understand that his destination was right next door to Mrs. Harrison. He looked in the street for the familiar vagrant, saw no one guarding the cars, stopped short of the Harrison house. This was ridiculous, quite ridiculous.

All he could recall for the moment was that woman's casual remarks about the affluence of them next door and the fat child of theirs he had once seen. Bitterness rose like bile, the heartburn of anger. Affluence, inexact anagram of flatulence, diminishes, ruins, desensitizes all those in possession, but above all else, pro-

tected them from evil, Amen. There could be nothing wrong with this house. He passed the Pearson Thorpes' slowly. Lights in each window, no need to worry about the quarterly bills, not they, what with no one in sight but, sitting like a king, one grand and perfect Persian cat slightly above the level of his eye, fitting height for his majesty occupying the whole of a windowsill. The indifference of the cat basking in good fortune and obscene health stung John like a whip, bringing treacherous tears to his eyes while the animal neither blinked nor stirred under his scrutiny. A pedigree purring. John moved on.

The seven o'clock sky was even darker and those ominous trees flanking the large houses were respectfully still. Fifteen self-conscious steps (turning back only once to look at the cat), until he was level with another window affording a better view. Inside here, a glowing kitchen, the same place where he had once been surprised by a senior lady dressed in lace, sipping sherry while inviting him to bow to her regal wave. But currently in her place, a small, bright, dark-haired boy with damson eyes, sitting in a high chair. Flowers on the table, big, fat, Michaelmas daisies. A man, so patently the father, cooked while the boy watched for the next meal, and a blond woman was setting their places, her face turned half to the light and a frown of concentration marring the features. You get to look old by doing that, John heard his own jeering words: watch for the frown lines, lady. There was a door at the far end beyond, only partially in sight, and greenery visible through large French windows beside. The boy at the table swayed to the sound of some music, waving a spoon in time to an orchestra which John, mere onlooker, could not hear.

He could not see the colors or the elegance, only the distance between these and other lives. Sod them. Sod the informer as well as this mother and child waiting like baby birds with ever open mouths. Sod them all. Bastards. Filthy rich, plutocratic, patrician, sound-proofed against youth and age, bastards. Deliberately he leaned over the railings, not so much careless of being seen as indifferent to their indifference, spat into the well of the basement, twice. He could write the fucking report blindfold; could describe in words stinking with authenticity each detail of every magnificent floor of this house, borrowing details, dimly remembered but still exact, from Mrs. Harrison's accounts of the house next door. "All

them stairs, Mr. Mills," her words taking him from room to room. He looked back once more toward the cat, so sure of its own survival, imagined the blond woman dressed in a fur coat. Threw the sweeties out of his pocket. Walked slowly and seething to an empty home.

The evening of the party posed all the normal problems. "What are you wearing?" Monica was asking Jenny, suspiciously bright with the evening of Tuesday.

"I don't know yet. Haven't finished putting the kids down. Can't think." She did not say the call was an intrusion, but her voice implied as much along with apology for her own irritation.

"Oh, that reminds me," Monica said, oblivious to the hint. "Did you have Katherine's kids at the weekend, like you said?"

"What? Oh, no, the older one had gone to stay with her grand-mother. Another time, I suppose. I was rather relieved, to tell the truth. Place is bedlam as it is. So I haven't thought of what to wear. It's only a few people for supper for God's sake."

"Well, I just wondered. Do we dress up or down, casual or smart?"

"Oh, I see what you mean. I'd dress up if I were you. Might prove a point. I will, I suppose, if you do. Besides, when have you ever seen Katherine casual at any kind of party?"

"Right. Out with the shoulder pads, heigh-ho. A total recon-struct in ten minutes. Should we take a present?"

"Yes. For Katherine, not for him. A not very exciting house plant, I thought." Jenny laughed, a guilty sharing of the undertone of malice which went against conscience but was worth the friend-ship resuming an even keel. If there were any question about division of loyalty, she was Monica's second and had been anxious about the whole evening. Then she remembered to telephone the American couple who had asked for directions, since last time they had lost themselves on the way, as they would this time, directions or not. For that purpose alone, they set out early.

Inside the Allendale kitchen, David put the finishing touches to the table. The surface of the wood was covered with an antique linen cloth (they had debated about that, Katherine preferring the texture of the wood but he preferring dignified protection), the

cutlery heavy silver, similarly old, bishop's pattern, and on each elaborate plate setting was a matching linen napkin, white embroidery on white, stiff as sails. In the center was a round dish of flowers, late blooming garden roses cut short to crowd against each other in a shallow pyramid of red and cream, dark-green foliage spilling on to the cloth. David loathed arrangements which ebbed and swayed, obscuring one person from another like the wispy ferns of restaurants. The lilies Katherine had arranged stood on one side, illuminated by two broad candles which would be placed with the final flourish on the table. The door to the garden stood open, the lawn smelling sweetly of the earlier rain which curtailed the idea of outdoor play since he could not have borne to see high heels sinking in the grass, but in the living room, drinks were ranged in the old and priceless tantalus, bottles gleaming in rows on either side. Katherine stayed there, out of the kitchen, hearing from where she stood the music playing as David worked, compact-disc music lifted from the studio to replace the workaday radio. Jeremy slept. Husband and wife were casually dressed, Katherine downstated in khaki skirt and blouse with no ornament other than a gold collar, broader than the wedding band on her finger but soft and comfortable, a new gift. She stayed in the drawing room because of the cool and the absence of rich smells, and besides in the living room, her room, she could survey her own work with a modicum of pride. Such high polish there was in here, such a multitude of colors in harmony. Sitting on the extreme edge of the striped sofa, she longed for the oblivion of sleep while her mouth craved soft-boiled eggs and bread soldiers, childish food with heavily sugared tea.

No such simple fare visible in the kitchen; basic ingredients and pans out of sight as all eight guests arrived with gratifying punctuality. They drank Tanqueray gin laced with minimal tonic and wedges of lemon, Glenfiddich whiskey with nothing, Sancerre or dry fino, each couple perversely varying their favorite tipple, all generously administered to accompany smoked oysters on ivory cocktail sticks and tiny rounds of red-roe covered pastry. While Sebastian Pearson Thorpe fascinated the American wife with his sandy Anglo-Saxon looks and artless public-school accent, Monica, splendid as a peacock in pink and black, made very merry with Jenny's husband, and Jenny spoke to Colin with similar

animation. Both women were ceasing to notice how, in comparison to their hostess, they were somewhat overdressed and forgetting that fact was going to take far more of the white wine. Jenny observed without anxiety the passing of a lingering glance from Colin across the large room, over the bold stripes and colorful cushions she so admired, toward the armchair where Katherine sat, sipping fruit juice, as delicately fragile as David, incongruously perched on the arm, was solid. Monica had taken the second glass before they all moved across the hall to ooh and aah the table: Susan Pearson Thorpe merely her first since they were late; David inconspicuously drank his small, but third whiskey. Merely imagining the tension of hosting, from which her own sufferings were always extreme, Jenny allowed a moment's sympathy. Her eyes were drawn to his hard body: she found it impossible not to imagine him *in flagrante,* naked as a baby but rampant as a bull, wondered what shape he was, turned away in embarrassment and watched the rest. All of them vaguely familiar from similar occasions, in this house or other houses, weeks or months since, plenty enough acquaintance to justify them all greeting with loud familiarity. As if they were friends. That was the conspiracy. They were bound, seduced and easily persuaded to applaud one another: mutual approval the purpose of the evening with which all present willingly complied. But the small element so vital to such an occasion, a sort of spontaneous burst of relaxation, goodwill or whatever ingredient, was missing. There was in progress during those initial stages, too much of watching and impressing, too many darting eyes.

By the time all sat at table and the candles were lit, they were noisy perforce and some sense of genuine celebration took over. It was the table itself, so beautiful, an aesthetic appetizer for the food to follow. Each was supplied with a battery of glasses. Small portions of cold artichoke soup, served with a little sherry. "No, we did not grow the artichokes," David apologizing manfully, "did we, darling? I'm afraid to admit this is a tribute to the delicatessen. One simply adds the cream." Who is *one?* Monica wondered: I would have thought Katherine did all the cooking, remembering at the same time he was no mean hand with a pot or pan: even for a lunch of cold roast beef with fresh horseradish sauce. Good God, he might have done it all: so why had she ended up married

to Colin, who did so much less and did not always do it well. She felt a little bitter, ate more swiftly than the soup deserved. Susan Pearson Thorpe, far more muted than Jenny remembered, but charming, perfectly charming to the Americans, spooned the creamy mixture into her mouth with what seemed genuine hunger while the rest were more delicate. At the same time she had swallowed the alcoholic accompaniment in a single gulp, looked at the empty glass in mild surprise. David talked about food. In fact, they all talked about food. Sebastian recollected some uncle of his saying that the brandy and cigars formed the more spiritual part of the meal and he was glad to reflect that the two temporal ingredients were bound to be forthcoming, and discussion of grub was bound to cease. Susan and he should do more of this. He ventured a smile in her direction, noticed she was trying so hard part of him melted. The day had not been easy: she might have wished to see herself transformed, but he really did not want her like a Katherine. Depending on this evening's restraint, he would tell her so.

"You really need to go to the eastern seaboard if you guys really like to eat," said the American, eyeing the next course, noting with great approval a dish of sole véronique. "If you like fish," he added. "I just happen to love fish, any kind of fish." "Especially lobster," his wife added. "He goes crazy over lobster." "Have you had any oysters this year?" said Sebastian so politely he sounded like an advertisement. "Season just begun, I believe." "Oh, oh," joked the American wife, "fun and games in the shires, I guess. I just couldn't let him eat oysters. Is it really true, I mean, what they're supposed to do to you?" She addressed the question to her host, enjoying herself. David winked roguishly. Katherine cleared plates with delicate and almost noiseless efficiency.

Schools: they were on to schools. Sebastian liked this better than food or furnishings, both of which might have offended his wife, but he still looked forward to something else. Which schools and where, horses for coarses, a loud pun from Monica which made him wince. At least Susan and he were in agreement on this front; knew which paths were surfaced for their children, added them into the conversation. "What about Jeanetta?" Jenny asked, a question over her shoulder in a polite attempt to include monosyllabic Katherine and make her belong. "Where will she go?"

"What? Oh . . ." A plate dropped from her hands and crashed

to the floor, followed by a chorus of cheers, sympathies and offers to help. "Oh, don't worry," said David, "always happens. Wasn't a very special plate, no, no, sit down. Darling, can you pass me the serving spoon?" "Will you look at that," said Jenny, the wonder again so genuine she was pointing with one finger as if the rest could not see exactly what she saw. Slices of duck, overlapping in a rich circle on a dish, stewed cranberries as centerpiece and the table full of the scent of both. "How do you get a duck to behave like that?" said the American, impressed. "My, oh my," said his wife, sitting on David's right as David transferred slices on to plates and she passed them along with the aid of her linen napkin. Katherine fussed with a dish of tiny French beans and a platter of duchesse potatoes which other hands took from hers. On the sideboard by the lilies, a magnificent glass bowl of salad had appeared, radicchio glowing purple, Monica noticed, lifted from the fridge early to remove the chill. The next course settled as they ate the last. Inevitably, the conversation returned to food.

Where do you buy cranberries, how do you cook like this, where do you get the best fish, poultry, game, questions all smothered in sauce. The compact-disc player had stopped in reverence as mouths filled in preparation for a further round of compliments and questions, leaving one whole minute of masticating silence. Two glasses were empty, the quiet not uncomfortable since all bar Katherine were eating with concentration. Monica began to talk again first, but as David passed around the back of the high-backed chairs with the wine, his hand brushed her shoulder and she forgot what she wanted to say. Colin knew: it was something about the duck, part of an old argument, but he remembered not to speak when his mouth was full. And then into the continuing semi-silence, each of them in turn heard the sound of scratching.

Colin noticed first and turned his head. Monica looked at him inquiringly, taking the direction of his gaze. Then Jenny and then the American wife. Sebastian took no notice, concentrating on his food, and Susan Pearson Thorpe, finding the whole evening desperate, was raising her glass. The scratching came from beyond the playroom door at the far end of the room, a slight but regular sound, almost like the sawing of wood heard from a distance. Monica thought immediately of the similar sound made by a puppy she once had which would scrape at a door, scrape, scrape, pause

to wait for some sort of reply, surprised that the door would not shift, repeat the process, scrape, scrape, sit back on haunches. "What on earth is that, David?" she asked casually, none of them in any sense alarmed, merely curious. "Sounds like a dog."

He had put down the wine and crossed the room to the compact-disc player, flicked one or two switches so the music recommenced, slightly louder, putting his napkin to his mouth. "Pardon?"

"I said it sounded like a dog. In there." He laughed easily. "No, no, no. Not a dog. Kittens, actually, for the children. We keep them in the . . ." he flourished with his hand, still holding the napkin. "In the playroom," Monica finished for him. She had the habit of finishing sentences for others, a trick Colin loathed. Now he looked at her curiously. He had not known the Allendales had anything designated as a playroom: it was somehow out of character. "Kittens!" The American wife clapped her hands. The sound was friendly but sudden and as she stopped, the same scratching sound was still slightly audible. "Oh, I love them, the darlings, can we see? Oh, come on, David, give us a peek."

"No, not now. They run up the walls, you see . . ." He began on longer explanations, but the words were not finished. With an indelicate choking sound, Katherine had half risen, pushed herself back from the table, and was suddenly, monstrously sick. She was sitting at one end of the table, opposite David, and the hands, gripping each corner within reach, clutched at the edges, her fingers so white the rings glowed against the cloth, while highly colored, undigested, viscous food splashed to the floor, the remnants dribbling from her mouth. All of them watched her head thrown forward, the bright-blue eyes staring at the playroom door beyond. Then all eyes turned to the mess on the floor, a solid fluid of brilliant colors. Until David moved, nimble as a fighter around a ring, lifted her bodily out of her chair and lightly flicked his fingers across her cheek. Lacking the brutality of a slap, the effect was the same and she closed her drooping mouth abruptly, beginning to cough. Tears had sprung to her eyes. "Shh, darling, shh. It's all right." She leaned into him, taking the support of his arms, but rigid. Like a ballerina, Jenny thought later, held tense by a partner in a *pas de deux*. David flashed his disarming smile on the assembly, who faced the tableau of himself and his wife with varying expressions of horror. "Excuse us," he said. "I'll explain in a minute. Please,

carry on." Both left the room. Susan Pearson Thorpe heard them going upstairs, David's soothing tones floating back.

"Katherine never did like cats," she observed. Monica sniffed nervously, slightly comforted by the remark which none could regard as anything but poor taste. It made her want to giggle. She and Jenny quickly found cloths and scooped the mess off the floor, both used to dealing with children, pragmatic while the men looked on, dumbly. All of them had lost appetite, but there was nothing else to do but finish the food. At least the food on the plates. No one would have wanted to ask for more.

They were all waiting for the return of the host, all privately planning when they should leave.

"Listen," said Jenny, "I think I should go and help, really."

"Perhaps not," said Monica. "I'm sure David knows what to do. It seems to have happened before." Colin nodded agreement. Jenny put down her napkin. "Well, in that case he can tell me to mind my own business." She rose. Monica rose too. "I'll come as well." "I won't," said Susan, "I would be *de trop*." They went upstairs, neither sure of where to go, looking inside two rooms before they found the third, signaled by David leaving, pulling the door to behind him. "She's all right," he said reassuringly. Jenny pushed past him, suddenly determined. "Well, could I just say goodnight, then? Perhaps a woman could help, you know." He hesitated, nodded to let them go in, but hovered at the door. Katherine lay on one side of the double bed, covered with a quilt, one knuckle in her mouth and her eyes open. "What is it, Kath, what is it? Better now?" Jenny murmured as she would to the youngest of her children suffering from a scratch. Katherine was trying to speak, touched Jenny's hand with the fingers taken from her own mouth, damp with saliva, an unpleasant touch, but the words were incoherent.

"Please," said David from the door, "please don't. You'll only get her excited." Monica felt pity rise, along with a tinge of revulsion. "I've got some valium," she said. "Would that help?" David looked at them both as if toward saviors. "Oh yes," he said, "it would. She usually has some, but forgot to get more. She's pregnant, you see: it does this . . ."

"No valium, then," said Jenny firmly. "Oh no, the doc says it's fine . . . It was for me," said Monica, fumbling in the handbag

which accompanied her everywhere. The news of pregnancy had a strange effect on her, like a slap or a sharp punch. "Half of that, then," Jenny insisted. "She's only small." The eyes on the bed followed their movements, drank water, looking toward Monica in something akin to fear, toward Jenny in a plea she refused to register. The mouth stopped mumbling and swallowed without resisting. After five minutes, they went downstairs, leaving the door open. In the kitchen the men had begun to smoke. They presumed they were not going to reach the spiritual part to the meal.

David resumed the role of host, pressed them to eat. She would want this, he said: she was so looking forward, please do. I'm afraid this sometimes happens with Katherine, her nerves. And she is in a certain condition, worries her so, the other two were not easy. Better in the morning. The men nodded wisely, full of sympathy, moved to kindness but feeling their own impotence and their own immunity. Susan Pearson Thorpe was silent, her glass half full but treated with indifference instead of the customary anxiety, while her look expressed extreme puzzlement as if she were working out a sum in her head. They accepted coffee, all of them, black please, without sugar, and were glad to go home. Monica Neill and Colin were breathing evenly as they got into their car, neither able to confess to the other how they had been worried for anything Katherine *in extremis* might have said. How good, they agreed, is David, what a shame for his birthday, pity. The Pearson Thorpes walked home. Jenny drove, and the Americans got lost en route, following them so far. All couples, still sober and in need of comfort, made love in their different, broadly similar fashions. They tried to forget the scratching and the shining, vomit-filled face in an exercise which lasted from five to thirty minutes, depending on who they were.

Equally occupied, but with a far greater degree of concentration, Mary Fox arched and crouched over the recumbent form of brown Claud, seeking the solace of sex for longer than all the rest of her sister's guests put together. They had wasted, after all, one whole hour before she had been convinced of his explanations, Katherine's total lack of involvement, which she already believed, only established after a very lengthy row. Ending inevitably in bed, him

with license to play until 11:30 in the evening. Claud did not tell the whole truth: Claud never did any more often than she expected and only then on subjects of no personal interest, but the half-truth he told was both recognizable as such and sufficient for her purpose. Wife ill, children ill, holiday postponed: don't be such a fool, if I'd been with anyone, it would not be anyone so near to you. You know me better than that. While she hardly did, she felt convinced and above everything else in her life, Claud, in all his anonymity, gave her hope. She forgot all her boredom, the sense of desperation which had dogged his absence, made her own version of love like an Amazon. You are thinner, darling, said in admiration: he liked his women skinny, such words easy on her ear, they made love again. The voracity of it all made him slightly relieved to go home and Mary, for once in weeks, relieved to be alone. She smoked a rare cigarette, drank the last of the wine Claud had brought as a peace offering and found herself satisfied, warm and only a trifle broody. Thinking could wait until the morning, tomorrow was not going to feature much by way of work. This was after all the way she liked it best. After they went home, provided she knew they would return. Her sister, misjudged Katherine, came swimming into focus as Mary brushed her teeth, swam out again as she applied her avocado nightcream. All that could also wait until tomorrow.

Katherine staggered out to the bathroom mirror. The huge eyes which stared back at her were the eyes of a stranger, a very old woman. Not the child she had seen reflected in the morning: there would never be a child reflected in this face. All an illusion, this sense of safety. She was an old woman, not allowed to go back in time. Downstairs was the child and the man who was murdering them both.

"Well, why should she behave like that, why?" Jenny had attempted to debate the Allendale behavior patterns with her husband on the way home and then again in bed. The first attempt had been futile: the second met with better response since he was mellow but tired enough to fall into sleep after the second paragraph. Compassion, such as it was, remained Jenny's contribution to family life along with concern and neighborly kindness: he

wanted no part of either and besides, there was work tomorrow. Stupid idea to have a dinner party on a Tuesday: you could tell how many people never really worked or they would know that Wednesday followed. Jenny was accustomed to such shutting off and could not argue with a man who was to all intents and purposes, bar the breathing, dead. She courted the same state in self-defense, thinking ahead to the day after and the few after that. But almost as soon as sleep intervened, the little one, Emily, came to wake her. Their bedroom door was shut and in reaching for the handle, Emily bumped and scraped on the bottom panel with the doll she carried. Jenny hardly registered the sound until the child stood by the bed, feigning distress but really wanting to play, pursuing no nightmare but lack of company. Theirs was a big bed: she could never see why she should not share. Jenny knew she should follow the books, get up herself and make the child resettle to ensure herself an easier long-term life, but she let Emily clamber beneath the duvet instead, sure that the other half, whose objections were always more strenuous, was in no position to notice until morning. Dolly was abandoned on the floor. As child fell back into sleep, Jenny remembered the scraping at the door, the dyspeptic duck and the kittens which had heralded the dinner party fiasco. The memory, along with indigestion, was profoundly disturbing. She hugged Emily close for comfort and vowed to do something tomorrow.

David cleared the kitchen systematically to the sound of the *1812* overture, suitably triumphant for the time of night. First he assembled all the glasses and washed these in soapy liquid, rinsed them in clear, hot water and stood them on towels. Neither glasses nor silverware could be entrusted to the dishwasher and Katherine would polish tomorrow. All other crockery was rinsed and stacked in the machine. He left behind him on the table a tray with all the bishop's pattern cutlery. Although slightly angry at the early demise of his evening, the irritation was gone and he regarded it as more of a success than failure, whistled idly as he worked, not in tune with the music which moved from one crescendo to another. Mechanical tasks, conducted with precision, pleased him: he could subdue to these the whole of his concentration, filling the sink with more hot, soapy water for the remaining silver. Wash, rinse,

stand upright like the glasses, no shortcuts to the final shine. What mollified him most about the evening was the way the table had glowed, the gasps of admiration almost orgasmic: David had liked that, a seal of approval for all those lovely things, arranged with care. He had never wanted anything which other people did not envy: there was no point. Nothing ugly after Daddy, nothing fat, nothing unsafe. Daddy tidying up like this after a bout of rage was something which had long since passed from mind. Turning to the table to fetch the last cutlery, he was pleased to notice out of the corner of one eye that the cloth had not been stained, only rumpled. More so than before.

By Katherine's hand, bunching a corner of heavy cloth into her left fist. She was paler than the color of the material: her other hand held a carving knife and she had been moving on her bare feet toward his back, the right hand raised, her face serene with determination, the thin body still dressed in crumpled skirt and blouse, the gold collar twisted around her neck. Two feet, three feet, progress steady, dragging the cloth after herself. "Now, now, darling, don't be silly." Cutlery clattered to the floor, released from the cloth which she seemed quite unable to relinquish. "Now, now," he repeated carefully, but she still came on with an even pace. The knife was sticky with the grease from the duck: the dirt offended him. David retreated almost into the sink, risked turning his back for one whole second. He lifted the half-full washing bowl, flung the contents in her direction.

The *1812* crashed to a finale.

21

SOPHIE WAS LEARNING CUNNING FROM HER CAT, A CREATURE WITH many other advantages. Kitten kept at bay all those vast wastes of insomnia which had led to such exhaustion, and because he, she, or it appeared to grow by the minute, mimicking the antics of a lion at play with a lot of delightful running and snarling, Sophie had convinced herself that the presence of the cat would deter any burglar who was not a giant. "You just growl at him, dear," she said in admiration. "You know, the way you do when I pretend to take away your food. Oh, look at that, kitty, you were spitting. Ever so fearsome. Was your mother a tiger, then, must have been. Funny color, though." Sophie giggled, watching the kitten stalking a ball of wool. "No sense of smell," Sophie scolded. "You can't tell pink from white."

Granny was aware that she talked to herself and the cat more than to anyone alive, pushed the thought out of her mind. There was no one else more thoroughly disposed to listen when she was frightened much of the time, and the cat seemed so fearless, as well as providing every excuse to delay her departures from the house and hasten her own return. This morning she had contemplated taking kitty to the hairdresser; she could not see why on earth they should mind, but some dull instinct told her that they

would. So she stayed at home, becoming vague on the subject of the hour, even vaguer than she was on what day of the week. Her memory slipped out of gear with such ease, as it had done for more than a year. Nobody seemed to notice or mind while she dwelt for much of the time in a tunnel of apprehension she could not confess, but beginning with the brainstorm which had made her pick up the cat, the selectivity of her recollection no longer dismayed her.

She concentrated on doing as she pleased, shedding onerous tasks whenever she wished. David's face, David's figure, never quite became blurred, but the thought of him and his wife and his children was a profound pain in her chest which was only cured by picking up the cat and cradling it. She did so now. "Should have gone," she said to the cat, "should have gone, you know, for his birthday. Only he wouldn't have you indoors, you should see what he does to cats." She pointed to the wall with her spare hand and held the fingers as if they were a gun. "Bang, bang. And anyway, he didn't ask, so he doesn't get a present. Lovely socks, silly boy." The luminous pink socks were sitting on the sofa beside her, along with a number of other items, only the socks garishly wrapped with the sellotape very prominent, making the whole parcel gleam stickily. "But Jeanetta would like you, she would so. We'll go tomorrow."

When the phone rang, she was reluctant to move. The afternoon sun was so pretty through the window and the kitten had gone to sleep on her lap. With a slight start, she realized she was not wearing a skirt, only an underslip, which was why the kitten felt particularly warm and tactile and the juvenile claws so sharp. The thought of being caught thus, in a state of *déshabillé*, made her move. Remembering the phone was only the phone, not attached to a television, slowed her down again and she did not answer with the alacrity which had once been her hallmark.

"Sophie? Is that you?" Sophie turned and grimaced at the cat, which sat at her feet, discomfited and looking for entertainment.

"Course it's me. Who else would it be?" Sophie smoothed the pieces of fur from the underskirt, noticing without caring that the fabric was grubby. The sight of her own hair in the hallway mirror over the phone was not encouraging either, so she simply moved away. There was a little difficulty remembering the voice on the

other end of the line which was overfamiliar and one she did not like.

"How are you, dear?"

"I'm not dear. I'm cheap. And I'm fine. Thank you." Mary Fox, never the most sensitive, began to appreciate the call was not entirely welcome. "Oh, good," she said, lost for words. "Listen, won't keep you, you must be busy . . ." Sophie nearly spat down the phone. Of course I'm busy.

". . . Did you go and see David and Katherine? Like you said?" The voice always assumed this sort of wooing she had never realized she could not abide. Not at all like Katherine, who listened rather than spoke, although you wished all the time she would.

"No. I spec they had a party, they usually do. I didn't go around. They'd be clearing up. Changing the towels. I know I said I would go, but then I thought I wouldn't. Mustn't impose," she added meaningfully. My word, the wits were sharp today, she'd cut herself. There were no cares left in the world: only annoyances. "Just checking," said the voice. "Any other news?" Sophie hesitated, not yet immune from the desire to speak. "We . . . ell, I didn't get my hair done. They wouldn't let me bring the cat." Mary paused at the other end of the phone, breathed out slowly. Another one for the social services. "All right," she cooed, "see you soon."

Sophie went into her bedroom and put on a skirt, the brightest she could find, covered in mossy roses and flimsy for the time of year. Then she turned on the radio and settled down.

Right, right, action stations. Mary was not used to guilt, found the sensation acutely uncomfortable. It was all after waking with that unaccustomed stiffness of limbs which created the sensation she had spent half her life avoiding: introspection rampant as she rolled out of bed very carefully and very late, one foot moving after the other in slow motion to the bathroom. No conscience about the lovely sex which had created such complaints among the joints, the removal of the sticky diaphragm from between her thighs a positive pleasure, but guilt on the subject of sisterhood, suspended from the night before to return like a hangover and play havoc with breakfast. Mary phoned Child Action Volunteers. There was no real anxiety about Katherine's children: there never had been on her part. Yes, they had had the report since Tuesday

afternoon and could say now there was nothing wrong, absolutely nothing: Mr. Mills had been quite emphatic. Would she like to enlarge, for the record, why she had thought there was? No she would not. Mary felt guilty about asking for that shabby man. Not a serious guilt on that score. Any bossy intervention minimized guilt, but somehow it had returned in dragon shape the next morning. So in the afternoon, having failed to digest the beast, she phoned first Sophie and then David. She was mildly alarmed by the first call, infinitely more so by the second.

"Hallo, David. Mary here. Happy birthday for yesterday." She could not resist a small hint about being excluded from any celebration. Duty had dictated she send him a card, which he did not mention.

"Thank you," he said.

"Katherine there?"

"No, as it happens. Gone to the gym."

"Should she?" Mary bit her tongue, not wishing him to guess any secondhand knowledge she might have about Katherine's alleged condition since she sensed David would not approve this clandestine contact with his mother. "Why not?" said David. "She finds it helps with the tiredness. I made her go. Such a lovely day."

Made her go. This caused Mary to bristle: so did the fact he did not say, How are you, not seen you in ages, so bloody impersonal as befits a mere spinster sister. They would see: her blood was up. "Kids okay?" she persisted.

"Fine, fine. Jeanetta's staying with her granny."

The last information was dispensed without any great enthusiasm, a piece of news often repeated, so much so that Mary almost took the statement at conversational face value, until her heart missed a beat and her hand clutched the receiver in mute recognition of a downright lie. Instinct forbade her to contradict. "Oh. What time is Kath due back?"

"Don't know really. Five-ish. I'm spring-cleaning just now."

"I'll be around then." To leave no possible chance for an excuse she replaced the phone as soon as she spoke, stood there, shaking with anger, then looked at her watch. Three-ish. Go now.

Mary always knew the way to everything: Katherine did not, but the route she followed that afternoon was followed blindly.

THE PLAYROOM

She had been told to go out so she was going out. There was no hope for anything unless she did exactly as she was told and she had no will to do anything else. Down road, cross road at zebra crossing one hundred yards on left, take train at one of two possible tube stops, or not if she fancied waiting for the bus, which she did not since movement was a must and standing still for all that uncertain time absolutely impossible, so she walked to Edgware. Got on one train then another, led by the same familiarity, clutching the bag which contained all the things for the gym, ready packed as ever. Went down the steps to the place, changed for mid-afternoon class half an hour early, smiling the same smile at mostly the same people. But all that precious orientation went when she started to move: the music's pulsation seemed not to reach the ears or if it did, to enter each orifice out of sequence in order to jumble in the middle, her mind fixed on sounds more rhythmic than heavy beat. In the studio mirror, she noticed her hair was lank, dulled by washing-up water which would not quite dry, patted and soothed her own locks with one uncertain hand while the others shook their legs. Then she participated as best she could. Stretch, flop, obey orders, at first roughly following the routine but gradually slipping further and further away, lagging behind or speeding in front. The class went on, each of them staring fixedly in the mirror to avoid looking at her, preternaturally pale, thin girl in the front corner, lacking any sense of coordination whatever. A newcomer smiled secretly to her friend, eyes raised to ceiling with a Look at that, we aren't so bad after all, who does she think she is? The friend shhhed her. Classes were slightly sacred, interruptions not popular, and if anyone could not take the pace they usually left and besides the occasional weirdo was not unknown. Classes included manic anorexics, hyperactive fatties and others more obviously in a world of their own.

Only when Katherine began to dance all by herself with a particular if clumsy grace, skittering across the floor with her arms in the air and her ballerina legs all over the place, did serious alarm set in. She sidestepped the barre, flung one ankle across with agile ease and lowered her chest to her knee with such abandon they could hear the sinews creak, removed the offending leg, replaced the other, removed that and danced on into high kicks, the rest jogging on the spot in time to the music, goggling with embar-

rassment. Then she twisted and fell heavily, stayed where she was. The beat was drowned in the sharp intake of breath, the sudden paralysis which was not broken until the teacher turned off the music and called for help.

They put a dressing gown around her shoulders and led her away. Babies, she kept on saying, I must have more babies. "But you already have two, Katherine, don't bother about it for now," said one of the mothers who knew the vague background details from changing-room chat where all mothers at least remembered the names and ages of each other's children as well as remembering to compliment each other on any loss of weight. "Babies," repeated Katherine; "I've only got one." "Two," the mother corrected. "You always told me you had two." "One," Katherine repeated vehemently. "Only one. Just one. I want to go back to the class." Spoken while the remnants of the class stood around her in a group of leotarded dummies, gaping at the code of words which only the mother could begin to understand. When Katherine was finally beyond her burbling speech, they decided the blanket was not enough and called for a doctor. Someone looked in her purse, surprised to find no money bar one fifty-pence piece, no trace of an address and nothing to define this woman at all.

David was indeed spring-cleaning. Mary could see that at once since she recognized all the symptoms and they were difficult to miss. He had led her into the kitchen only when her insistence on the doorstep grew louder and louder, having tried to shut the door on her with politeness: with equal insistence she had repositioned one foot and remained as she was, repeating how she would come in and wait. All right, he grudged, not long though, I'm busy. Shut the door behind you. Intent on following the sound of a radio speaking a play, Mary merely pushed the front door with one foot, the leg behind the foot still stiff. Katherine would be home soon, no matter if the door did not actually slam and some half-formed feeling in her preferred it not to be tightly shut.

She noticed on first sight how the contents of the cupboards were out on the floor and surfaces were covered with detritus from other regions of the house. Three gray plastic sacks were stacked by the sink: protruding from one were the heads of lilies, browned

to imperfection but far from dead. "Why are you chucking these?" Mary asked. "Plenty of life in them yet."

"Past their best," David said cheerfully, the smile on his face masking visible irritation. "Look, I'm in the middle of this . . . sorry about the mess. Do you want to come back later, when my wife, Katherine, I mean . . ."

"I'll wait," said Mary. "I'll help if you like. I'm good at this."

"No," he said violently.

"Well you can make me a cup of tea then and I'll watch." She was mildly surprised when he complied. Not even mere compliance but a fury of fuss with a china teapot, tea left to infuse while lovely Italian china mugs were banged out of a cupboard which he had to unlock. "Why lock it?" she asked, but he smiled the vacant smile of a polite and busy man. "Oh, children, you know." She imagined she could detect a slightly demonic gleam in his eye and for the moment she was frightened, but only for a moment. Fortified by tea and harmless chat on the subject of spring-cleaning, the brink of autumn, the weather, the removal of beetles from carpets and so forth, all of which he debated with animation. "Leaves drift indoors, and we must beware of harvest mice too," she finished ironically, determined to keep the upper hand and also to tease him. "Anyway, I thought Katherine would have done all this." "Sometimes," he replied vaguely. She took the plunge. There were several things she did not wish to say but felt obliged to say, all of them in private before Katherine came home.

"David. Where's Jeanetta?"

"Jeanetta?" His head turned on his neck toward hers as if he had difficulty placing the name. "Oh, Jeanetta. Staying with her grandmother. For the moment."

"Sophie?"

"Yes of course."

"Since when?" He looked at the table and passed his hands over the steam rising from his mug, at the same time pulling a mat beneath it to protect the table surface. "Only yesterday. We had a birthday party, you see." Mary felt her shoulders lift in relief; only since yesterday and Sophie this morning had forgotten to say, naughty Sophie. The relief was short-lived: Sophie would have said, even Sophie on the brink of senility would have burst forth with such tidings. Mary held her tongue and sipped her tea.

"Not your favorite child, is she?" she asked. David's eyes traveled to the open French windows. Outside on a small patio, Jeremy played with bricks, a study in childish concentration so acute he had neither noticed nor greeted his aunt.

"Jeanetta?" said David. He seemed unable to speak other than one-word questions, betraying an uncertainty, a man needing a prompt in the corner of his stage. "Jeanetta isn't mine, you know. Katherine's concern, that child." Ah, so that was it, an excuse for a dislike which might have nothing to do with what anyone would call real reasons, such as ugliness, lack of control, all features which Mary's casual and just occasionally acute perception had only now borne downwind, less the result of direct observation than the sum total of Katherine's offhand remarks. "Don't be such an absolute bloody fool," Mary shouted. "Of course she's yours, you crapulous idiot." Then she was quieter. People, even male people, were supposed to be amenable to reason and he was, after all, short on information. She was ready to inform but he went on, "She had this blond man, this lover when she met me. She saw him once or twice, you know, after she met me; she told me, she tells me everything. He was there, after we met, I know he was. After she was born, I kept waiting for Jeanetta to go dark, like Jeremy did, so soon, like me, but of course, you know who stayed pale and fat, like an albino. Of course she wasn't mine. Too ugly. Like a little pig. Blond pig."

Mary drew breath slowly and spoke with emphasis, as if speaking to an idiot. "Katherine had several lovers, which you must know very well." She was extremely precise to keep her temper and control the heat of her face. ". . . Including the last, one with the impossible name of Claud, a man inherited by me. In all senses. Claud is a man with a ten-year-old vasectomy if you must know, and you clearly must. He couldn't have produced a child if he'd tried. And he still tries. Are you listening?"

"Well, well, well." He was smiling and this time, she was more than slightly afraid but again the feeling passed. He shrugged and spoke with deliberation. "What a slut you are, Mary, must be in the family. Fancy screwing a man who can't make babies, I shall never understand women. Well, well. Too late now. Nothing to do with us, really, nothing at all. You-know-who was simply disgusting. She had to go. She was . . . Oh I don't know."

Was, was, was. The words registered like hammers, each striking a blow of different magnitude.

"She, you-know-who, Jeanetta, is not disgusting. You pig." Mary did not know she was screaming. "And anyway, where is she? Not with your mother."

He did not respond to the scream. "Look," he said with exaggerated patience, "look, I'm having this spring-clean and I've got to finish, you've got to go. Must clear the mess, can't stand it, Katherine can't stand it, such a heap . . ."

She leapt from the table and slapped him very hard. The combined force of guilt and rising hysteria were behind the slap, so sharp the imprint of her fingers remained on his face like a birthmark. Towering above him she stared down and watched a vague and dreamy look come into his eyes as he put one hand to his flushed cheek. "Don't," he said pleadingly, "don't, please."

"Where is your fucking daughter?" Mary said, her voice descending to a low hiss, her sharp face thrust into his. His glance drifted beyond her, over the gray sacks by the sink and swiveling around to the French windows and the playroom door. "Tell her, Jeremy boy," he said. "She wants to know." The boy, bored at last, staggered through from the garden with a broad smile on his face. He brought for his aunty three of the bricks and a key. On a key-ring, the jangling sound a source of better delight than any rattle. He did not want to let go.

"Show me," said Mary.

22

I THOUGHT I WAS GOOD AT SUMS. ANOTHER JOKE. AS IT HAPPENS I have been quite incapable of the most simple factual additions. So I think now. Tuesday night, prelude to a slow and uneventful Wednesday morning, was one of the first when I have retired to bed with only a modicum of alcohol aboard and I was not entirely sure I liked the result. Not with dear Sebastian, I mean: that was nice and waking up to find him, my feelings as uncertain as they are, is at least a qualified delight. Sometimes it is better not to think and taking refuge in the depressed jumble which weighs on post-alcoholic dawns might be preferable to the sharper focus of sobriety. At least when suffering from an overdose one never thought of anyone else; there was no room. But I woke today with other worries, a sort of indigestion from everything I had seen.

We should not have gone to the damned dinner party, would not have gone except for the guilt created by an invitation sent so long in advance and the knowledge of a small gathering where we would be missed: I have not quite lost my manners yet and some of them are returning. Then there was Mark, of course, insisting he would be all right because he wanted a break from his parents for the privilege of watching TV later than they would

allow, with the Harrisons. And Sebastian saying we ought, you know. Me fishing out a dress, such a novelty going anywhere with a husband and remembering how often I had refused in the past, grateful for the chance to redress and determined not to overdo the drink. I had not told Sebastian all about Katherine and our distrust: not about the necklace, for instance. There was a portcullis over my tongue which stayed down all evening and after we came home. So that two things haunted me well into today's sober dawn. Not her being sick like that, revolting though it was: I don't know why, horrific without being too surprising, but the necklace she wore, as solid a piece of gold as ever I saw, so why the hell did she need mine? Oh I know a thief is not selective on the basis of need, but why, when she could never wear the damn thing with one already. Unless of course, she took mine to sell. A gold collar like a prize slave-girl: poor Katherine: I found it in me to pity her even before she vomited all that lovely food. But more insistent than that, I was haunted by the scraping at the door, the funny sound which seemed to trigger the explosion, scraping and scratching by kittens. In that house, temple of cleanliness and germ free, with baby Jeremy allergic and her always trying to poison our cats? Impossible to believe whatever he said: they would never spend good money on kittens and I've never known any cat make a noise like that. I said as much to Sebastian and he said they probably kept monkeys. Without elaborating, he seems to have changed his favorable opinion of David Allendale. Never mind, said my spouse: none of our business. I wondered: remembered all those clothes outside and felt another chill in my bones. I don't often confide in Mrs. Harrison, but I told her about the party because she asked and I couldn't just say everything was fine. Hearing about the hysteria, she simply stared and shuffled, then burst forth. "We was so worried, Mrs. P, we got the NSPCC round to them . . ."

"You what?"

"We was worried about Jeanetta," she said defensively. "I did tell you."

"Yes," I said shamefacedly, "you did. But the NSPCC . . . Really! Did they go?" Her face was full of relief but she did not want to elaborate: the whole episode was obviously hideously embarrassing as far as she was concerned.

"So I gather," she mumbled. "I spoke to Mrs. Al'dale's sister: a man went about it. Nothing wrong. Anyway, Jeanetta's with her granny, so it was all a false alarm." I let it go at that, all of it festering in the same chill.

Oh well, Samantha's turn for treats today, to mollify the jealousy (this child is so like her mother), which is now extreme. She went out with her father alone for a heavy-duty tea, leaving Mark and I alone with the Junior Scrabble, him with the leg irritating like a scratch. Not exactly a treat for him, but I'm ashamed to say, one for me since so novel is this spending time with them, I'm still enthralled by it and I hope the feeling passes after a while or I might never go back to work. So clever, this boy, at games, he could almost let me win, but as if the distractions in my mind were infectious, he could not concentrate either. The Allendales were still percolating on the brain and I could not persuade them to take a graceful exit. When the dog scraped at the door to join us in the study, I jumped. Thought of trivial, unconnected things. Mark spelled out T H I E F with triumph. Memory does strange things, but I had forgotten his sleepy confessions.

"Mark, you remember telling me about the strange man, and Sammy saying he'd come back when you were away with Daddy?" He nodded. "I shouldn't . . ." he began. "Course you should, darling. Don't worry, I know all about it, but if he came last week, when was it he came the first time?" He saw no contradictions in these statements of my knowledge, frowned in an effort to remember.

"Oh, ages and ages. I know, yes I know. Jus' before Jeanetta and Jemmy stopped coming and stayed at home, then. I think. He came in when Mr. Harry and me was watching the cricket and Mr. Harry was telling me about cricket. Did you know, Mummy, a cricket ball can break your head?"

"The vagrant man, darling," I reminded, picking up my Scrabble pieces.

"Oh yes. We chased him out, Mr. Harry and me. He got in upstairs, then Mr. Harry heard him moving about so we chased him out. I wasn't scared 'cause I'd seen him before anyway. With you, out of the window, and another time." His voice went down to whispering level. "Mr. Harry thought he took something. He

was worried, but the man hadn't done nothing. Sammy says when he came back, he wanted to get in."

I am beyond anger these days, or that would have been uppermost in my mind, might have been, had I been more interested in control of my house than I was currently in the Allendales'. I had always known, after all, that the honesty of Mrs. Harrison is selective. A simple connection of memory hastened by the ever-present picture of Katherine with gold collar. An intruder in our house, not confessed to me, on or about the day that bloody necklace went adrift. Oh, poor Katherine: I could have misjudged so much more than I thought.

"Daddy'll be home soon," I said smoothly. (Nice, actually, to be able to say that.) "Then I'll go next door and see if Jeanetta's back. She might come in and play with you." And I make some kind of peace with her mother, I did not add. Mark's face lit up.

"You could go now," he suggested helpfully. In the eyes of an almost eight-year-old, adult company cannot compete with another child, even a far younger child.

I laughed at him. "All right. Mr. Harrison will come up. Don't get into mischief."

"I can't move," he sighed.

Neither could I, or at least not with any speed. I have ever been reluctant to enter the perfect portals of next door, because they put me to shame and my reaction to shame has always been resentment. In daylight or darkness, I do not like that house despite admiration, which is not the same thing. Which is why I paused to put lipstick on mouth and comb hair before leaving: sometimes these boosters have an effect, not always and not really today. So sunny and warm this street, an Indian summer now, merged with the last of the proper season, the trees shedding first and giving the only hint of future darkness. Mark says he can never believe it will get dark again, why should it, and I tend to agree. I still did not want to go and knock next door, even when I had made up my mind and got out into the road, I walked slowly like a sightseer. I went up the steps to their door; rehearsing a few words about thanking them for dinner and found as I raised a hand to the bell, that the door was just open. Oh good, that would break any ice: I could joke about our vagrants (there was a new one hanging

around in the street) and warn them to be more careful. Hate it when the door is on the latch like that: one never knows what to do. You can't push it open and go in unless you know the family well and otherwise you simply wait like a lemon or shout. I was trying to decide but I did not have the chance.

Screams, screams, more screams, emanating from the womb of that building, cutting around the door from the dark hole of the hallway and into my ears like knives. Katherine's screams, I thought: I had been imagining screams in my head for almost twenty-four hours, hated the reverberation which would not leave me alone, paralyzed me all over again. You cannot analyze screams, say on first hearing if they are anger, terror, fear, but they must always be fear, there is little else which matters in a scream. My God, these were endless and I was a coward. Mind your own business: you owe nothing: simply her pregnant nerves, their affair not yours. And then, it could be murder, might not be safe to go in there, you fool, you have children of your own and you want to live. Standing on the doorstep, looking around for help and seeing none: children in there too. You would kill a person who left one of yours in a house with screams like that. And you owe Katherine: she might be hurt: she's having a baby, she's fallen: go in, go in, you ghastly, drunken coward. Into the kitchen, following the path of the sound, so easy, no mistaking, first room off the hall, you were there not long ago. More screams in disharmony with the rest: a child, that boy Jeremy screaming with his mother. I ran the last few steps.

At first I thought it must have been murder, a fight of massive proportions, the pristine kitchen I had sat in and admired through their window a heap of junk, bags, bits everywhere, everything in comparative chaos, not the place of entertainment I had known. After his impression of violence, the next thing I registered was the howling face of the boy, standing by the French window un-attended, his face red with shrieking, holding a blue brick in one hand, frightened. I looked for Katherine, the source of the barking screams so different from those of the boy, saw what I took to be her until I realized in the same split second it was not, struggling with David in the door of the playroom. Sunlight streamed through, blurring his features, making her, this woman, a silhou-ette merged with his: they were not so much struggling as holding

on to each other, he preventing either of them moving, pushing her back away from the opening. Her face was turned to the sun: the struggle seemed absurd but still she screamed. They did not notice me and he pushed her clear of the door, saying something, his voice guttural with panic. The next thought of mine was relief: no one hurt yet, no blood, me interfering; nothing but noise: an argument and a terrified child, but then on a peculiar instinct less brave than curious, I slipped between the distracted adults and into the sunny alcove where the children played: their room, blinded by sunlight, seeking out each corner.

Such colors in there, such hideous, hideous mess. Clothes and dismembered toys, little teddy bear legs, broken cars and torn posters, but mostly clothes, shiny fabric, a large expanse of vivid purple cloth. Beyond that, a cloud of pale-blond hair, obscenely colored against the material, a half of a face visible and one small hand with huge knuckles. From the other end of the purple cloth there stuck a thin calf with a foot simply and pathetically adorned with one white sock. She did not move.

It was then they noticed me, the adults, or it may have been then he slapped her to stop the screaming, not a flick of the fingers this time, a slap. I knew by then she was not Katherine but I did not care, whoever she was did not matter. She appeared to subside in the brief glance I gave her, looking to David for some sort of explanation. But he shouted, was all: my eyes, still adjusting to the contrast of light and dark, only noticed a contortion of his face into a shout of furious warning, one fist clenched toward me, the other holding her. Only the threat went home, the danger. I turned back, instinct again, stopped, bent down, tucked the purple around the child on the floor, scooped her up and ran. Not running as I scarcely know how to run: running like Sammy did when she learned to walk, a drunken stagger, ungainly, effective, determined. Crashing through the front door into the street, up to our door, pressing the bell with my chin, the limbs of the thing I was carrying flapping around my waist, arms and legs free, the one white sock left on the pavement. A brittle, septic-smelling, bundle, damp against my blouse. Into our house past whoever opened the door, shouting myself, get this, get that, phone, phone, I can't remember, but I know it was coherent. Breathless, upstairs, shouting some more. He was behind me in the street, I know he was,

that man: he will try to get in. My voice screaming. Get Mark out of the way, and for Christ's sake, phone.

We sit with her in the study. I shall be sitting here forever in my mind. I thought my own trembling might communicate some movement, but not yet. Downstairs there is someone hammering on the door, voices raised, but too soon for all the help. I know who you are, my sweet: I knew as soon as I saw your hair and I sit here weeping for all my blindness while those around me organize. There is nothing more important than a little life, my own child or anyone else's, even if it were a life I ignored; why didn't I know, why didn't I see. What wickedness, what terrible stupidity. Bring the doctor, yes, yes. If I hold on to this child, I shall warm her. Don't do this to me, God, you bastard, can't you see I was learning already? There was never a more hapless, futile weeping, such harsh initiation into priorities. I must stop crying and hold still: tears fall chilly on this shiny cloth and God she needs the warmth. The face of her is familiar, but very, very old. I think in some weird flash of the futility of face cream. I must hold her tightly, so that she feels the radiant heat of me. Our silly adult lives do not matter, may she please have the choices we have got. Why didn't I see? He is shouting at the door, Give her back, she's mine, she's mine. I shall never give her back.

Sebastian will be here soon. They will all be here soon.

She is very cold.

23

MARY GOT UP FROM HER CHAIR AND CLOSED THE CASEMENT WINDOW of her bedroom with noisy efficiency. What had once been a bare boudoir was now cluttered, overfurnished with an armchair, clothes strewn carelessly but with some sense of order. Not a tip, to use Mary's own phrase, but not tidy either. Katherine was curled in the armchair, wearing a track suit of great antiquity, Mary's from more energetic days. The shiny magazine she was reading fell to the floor as she raised one hand to tuck hair behind her ear. The smile she gave Mary was dutiful, automatic, not quite reaching the eyes, but an attempt nevertheless. Mary was grateful for anything, felt the rising in her of a protection so fierce she wanted to place barriers on the door. Any expression, any concession to life, was preferable to the catatonic state of her sister when first she had walked upstairs. Katherine squinted toward the sunlight from the window, rattled by a gust of autumn wind outside. Her face became anxious and Mary felt alarm.

"What's the matter, Kath?"

"Those curtains need mending. The hems have all frayed. Can't have been very good cotton."

"Or very good sewing," said Mary tartly. "You made them, remember?"

"Did I? Oh yes. Liberty cotton. Remnants in the sale. You didn't like them. You wanted blinds."

"I love them," said Mary, stepping up on to a stool by the window and unhooking the material from the rail overhead, "so you'd better mend them, okay?"

"All right."

Now there was a triumph: little sister presented with a sewing box, looking into the contents as if they were not entirely unfamiliar. Slowly, with all the deliberate movements of a drunk, finding a needle and the wrong-colored cotton reel, threading the eye with enormous concentration. Picking up the first curtain, turning up the hem again and making great, clumsy tacking stitches. Really, Mary thought, it does not matter how they look.

"I made a whole bedspread once," Katherine said inconsequentially.

"So you did. Do you want something to eat, Kath? We never had any lunch." She ignored the shudder which shook her sister from neck to feet, the pale face impossibly paler as her head shook a faint negative. "Come on," Mary coaxed, "I mean, nothing much. Toast or something. Eggs and toast soldiers. You know very well that's the limit of my culinary skills."

"Bad for you," said Katherine automatically, "all that cholesterol. Just toast, if you're really making some."

"Milky tea?"

"Please." The hands were becoming more certain over their work and the tacking stitches were smaller and more precise. Thank God. Not out of the woods, Mary thought, but perhaps beginning to recognize the trees. She sat on the bed, wanting to fold the pajamas which were Katherine's apparel for most of the day. Striped and flannelette, Mary's again since Mary never threw anything away, resurrected and worn uncomfortably, Katherine's insistence. Katherine saw her sister looking at the pajamas and looking away.

"I know they make me look like a convict," she said calmly, biting the end of the thread. "All they need is little arrows on them. Don't worry, I'll soon be what I look like when I'm wearing those. Convict."

"Oh, Kath, stop it. The lawyer said, well he said, he doubted if . . ."

"I know what he said. I do have ears, you know." There was no shade of reproof in the tone. "He said it would depend on the charge, and whatever happens, they don't always put you away. And on what He says, of course." He. There were names they could neither of them mention, not even Mary in her newfound courage, her anxious, uncritical, guilty care. There had been a daughter and a father: now there was neither who could be described by forename, although their faces swam into focus with every passing thought. Confused, swollen, poisoned, hungry faces which made Katherine scream in the middle of the night. Mary, awake in unison, the two of them embracing in a way they had never before embraced, even as frightened children. "I love you, Kath, here lean on me, I'll try to do better," brushing away the lack of response, meaning every word. So humbling, to see how you had thought you knew someone, to find you had never known them at all.

"Oh well, I'll make this toast." Mary roused herself.

"If they do put me away," Katherine continued, determined to avoid the end of the subject which Mary so wished to block, "I shan't mind, you know, and you mustn't either. It would feel like paying a debt."

"That's no way to pay a debt. And I don't know how punishment comes into it. And we don't know yet if Jeanetta . . ."

"They'll be howling for my blood," said Katherine. "I know what people think. I read these magazines. I sometimes read your paper. There has to be punishment."

"You don't mean you won't even fight . . ."

"No," said Katherine, picking up the curtain again, stitching faster. "No, I don't mean that."

"Why, Kath, why? How did you let him?" Mary burst out.

"I wanted to go back," Katherine said. "Back to being little."

Mary left the room. She went into the kitchen to prepare some food. Katherine seemed to refuse eating in principle, but she could be persuaded toward the nibbling consumption of scraps. There were stocks of biscuits, sponge cake, cereal, bland carbohydrate, nothing fancier than eggs and Cheddar cheese, nothing which required the heating of a pan of oil or the scent of frying. The cheese was eaten with biscuits, the eggs were boiled, soup came out of a tin. Sophie's rations were on display, ready for a visit the

same afternoon, acting as both a relief and a trial, bringing the kitten in a special basket, the other arm holding a pint of milk and all conversation consistent of nothing but the rigors of her progress from her own house to this. In her merciful unawareness of all but unimportant detail, Sophie was even funny. Ha, ha, not much to laugh at at all, but then Mary's sense of humor had always been grim. Forbore even the visit of Mrs. Harrison with some of Katherine's clothes. Oh God, the quality of human kindness, like cruelty, was so strange, so completely unexpected. She had never known.

Katherine sat sewing, streamlining the pain of her thoughts by furious concentration on the stitches, stopping to look around the room. Spartan white walls, awful furniture, none of it as it had once been, offensive. The sort of semi-institutionalized room which was now synonymous with safety, devoid of character and containing nothing other than standard issue, brought in at a discount without thought of taste. She looked down at the cotton of the flimsy curtains. Some of it had made cushions too, she seemed to recall, pretty. Cushions like the sort you shoved down the front of your smock when you were about six, pretending to have a baby. Those were the days. Something from nothing. These were the days to follow. The room was hot, making a tiny trickle of perspiration escape from the line of her hair, forcing her to rise reluctantly and open the window cold-blooded Mary preferred closed. The flat was over a garden, with a road running along the side. Further down the road was a school and in the distance, newly released, childish voices were raised in screams, distant footsteps, distant taunts flying and thundering. Katherine closed the window, moved like an automatic toy back to the armchair, sat with eyes closed and heart pounding.

Something from nothing: nothing from something.

Sophie tiptoed in, still dressed in her coat, eyes alight with anticipation of tea and company. Seeing the eyes closed, she carefully placed the cat into Katherine's lap and stood back with satisfaction. She might know nothing else, but cats did things to people, look how. The thing mewed in protest, then simply accommodated itself to a new source of warmth. With a will all of their own, Katherine's fingers stroked the tabby fur. The cat began to purr and the sounds of the children began to recede from her mind.

"So you aren't dead then?" yelled Sophie. "Ah, curtains."

"No," Katherine said, kneading her hands gently in the neck of the animal on her knee. "Not dead. Not yet."

"Any news?" Sophie yelled again.

"No."

"Oh dear, dear me. Still, no news is good news."

The long fingers paused, tensed. "Why did you never warn me, Granny? About what he was like?"

Sophie shuffled. "He was only doing what was sort of done to us, dear. I didn't know he would. Don't let's talk about it now."

Mary came in with a tray of tea, weak to be laced with sugar.

"Where there's life there's hope," intoned Sophie, repossessing the cat. Katherine moved with a greater briskness, picked up the curtain again. "I knew a woman once," Sophie went on, "made her living out of sewing curtains." For the first time in the days of their resumed life, Mary saw on her sister's white face the ghost of determination.

"Well," murmured Katherine, "you may have just met another."

Then she began to cry, holding the printed cloth up to her eyes, a silent, soaking weeping.

Sophie turned away, hiding her distress. "I say," she hissed to Mary in a stage whisper, "they can't make her, you know, get rid of . . . it? Can they?"

"No, they can't." Katherine surprised them all by a loud voice, tremulous but almost shouting, petulant but determined. "They can't. I want it."

Wisely the woman kept silent. Mary smiled. They were safe here. Waiting.